Courage and Light Behind the Badge

W. Alan Orok

ISBN 978-1-64299-686-9 (paperback)
ISBN 978-1-64299-687-6 (digital)

Christian Faith Publishing, Inc.
832 Park Avenue
Meadville, PA 16335
www.christianfaithpublishing.com

This is a work of nonfiction.

The events and experiences depicted in this Book are all true and have been faithfully rendered as the Author remember them, to the best of his ability.

Some names and identities have been changed, however, in order to protect the anonymity or security of the various individuals involved.

Printed in the United States of America

FOREWORD

Courage and Light behind the badge details my own personal life involving 32 years of Law enforcement employment.

I've made the book to be a light-hearted story, sometimes involving humor which helped me cope with a stressful and dangerous job.

The average individual cannot cope nor survive Law Enforcement.

It involves my Christian perspective in viewing the tragedies that occur in everyday life.

It involves the men and women who patrol, protect and apprehend individuals who would otherwise harm us or our families.

ACKNOWLEDGMENT

Special thanks to: my best friend and soulmate, my wife Ika Orok for patiently schooling me in the area of computer skills and help in writing this book. Also for showing me what a great loving marriage is.

I also need to thank my mother, Catheline Orok. She showed me the gift of reading at a very young age.

Through buying numerous subscriptions to outdoor magazines I was able to hunt, fish and explore the world without leaving the comfort of home.

It got me to college and opened up a world of experiencing the lives of truck drivers, lawycrs, pilots and mysteries.

It opened the Bible and I got to know my Savior "Jesus".

To also express for the love I have for my two grown sons, Brian and Bradley. May your journey be safe, adventurous and productive.

CHAPTER 1

The Story Begins

Tyrone Johnson was raised by a single mother on the welfare system. He never met his father and was informed that his father was in prison somewhere. Tyrone had several siblings also with different fathers.

Tyrone was now thirty-two years old and was also living off the welfare system through several girlfriends.

He developed a dependency on crack cocaine when he was sixteen years old. The addiction owned him and was calling for him to obtain another "fix"—and soon. That meant stealing to obtain the required funds needed to purchase the drug. Tyrone had tried working several times, but that had required long hours and complete sobriety.

This would never work out for the fast talking "ladies man."

Tyrone loved breaking into cars. He was inside and gone within two minutes, taking electronics, phones, and sometimes, purses and wallets. Yes, people were actually stupid enough to leave these items in plain view.

"These chumps deserved to lose these items," according to Tyrone.

Tonight, Tyrone would score, and he would hurt anyone who tried to stop him. He did not fear the justice system. "What a joke." They always handed him a lenient sentence, and the medical benefits were excellent.

Officer Randy Smith was a thirteen-year veteran on the police force. Prior to police work, Randy obtained a two-year degree in police science, working part-time at nights. He applied in the San Jose police in 1980 and, after a year of numerous testing, was hired. The tests included physical, medical, background, and psychology tests.

Out of a thousand applicants, three were selected. Randy Smith was one of the three hired.

Officer Smith was married with three children. In addition to working forty to fifty hours a week in a patrol car, he also worked an eight-hour extra pay job as security for an apartment complex. This apartment complex had been receiving car break-ins during the evening hours. Officer Smith was thirty-five years old and had stood at 6'2" and weighed 250 pounds. Tonight, February 12, 1993, both men would meet.

The February night in San Jose, California was a mild evening and a clear night. The week had almost felt as if spring would be coming early this year. Tyrone had called a buddy named Willy to join him as they would drive in Tyrone's car and scout out parking lots for cars with items inside, which could be easily sold for money in order to purchase the "slave drug" crack cocaine. They passed several apartments in Blossom Hill Road until they passed one which they felt comfortable with.

Their plan was for Willy to approach a car and check to see if any of the cars were unlocked.

Tyrone would stay with the car to act as a look out. By viewing each car, they would look for electronic cords, which would indicate that an item of value may be hidden in the glove box.

They could also pull the lever to the trunk to see if any guns were being stored. Off duty FBI agents were notorious for leaving their weapons there. People made Tyrone's lifestyle very easy, and with his girlfriends on welfare, one had to be a fool to look for employment. If they had to smash a window, they made sure they were in and out within two minutes, leaving the area quickly. Tyrone kept a short baseball bat under his seat in case a victim tried to stop them.

Tyrone and Willy soon passed an apartment complex that looked promising. The lighting was not too bright, and most of the cars looked to be newer expensive cars, which would contain expensive items. Perfect.

Tyrone let Willy out of the car so Willy could canvass the area. Tyrone followed in the car and served as a lookout.

Willy's eyes lit up as he found an unlocked Lexus. The car contained a laptop computer, and a GPS unit was in the glove box. Tyrone opened his trunk to place the items in. The next car had a purse strap sticking out from underneath a towel. Poor Willy had to use a "slim Jim" devise to insert in the door in order to unlock the door. As soon as the door was opened, an alarm went off.

Officer Smith was approaching the parking lot and watched the black male adult jump into the passenger seat.

The officer stood in front of the car and raised his Smith & Wesson at the driver at a distance of about thirty-five feet and ordered the driver out. The driver instead accelerated at the officer and swerved the car directly at the officer. Officer Smith did not have time to jump out of the way. Officer Smith knew he would be run over. In a last second survival move and fearing he would go under the car, Smith jumped up onto the hood. He rolled off the hood and landed on his back. The impact jammed the magazine of the automatic pistol, rendering him unable to fire at the fleeing vehicle. Smith noted that the car was a 1970s Chevrolet Monte Carlo with a brown roof over a white body. The first three license numbers were 1DD.

Saturday morning, Feb 13, 1993

I was a detective for San Jose police and presently assigned to the missing persons unit. Although this usually required a Monday through Friday workweek, I requested to work Tuesday through Saturday.

I hated to come to work on Mondays and the fifty-five-minute commute to work was lighter on Saturday.

Although I mainly worked missing persons, I could be assigned to work in any area that the department needed me. I first began my day with briefing in Lt. Herman's office.

We went over the previous night's events had learned about Officer Smith's attempted murder with the suspect using his car to ram the officer. I also knew Randy Smith and had worked with him on occasion in the patrol unit.

My police business card read "Detective W. Alan Orok," but some people called me Al. Family and closer friends called me Alan. Payroll department called me by formal first name, William, which was on my time sheet. It did not matter; just do not call me "late for dinner."

I met with Randy at the officer's report writing room. He told me that he had jumped up high when he could not avoid the car. He felt he would be crushed if he went under, and I am sure that this move had saved his life. As a suspect, one thing you never wanted to do is harm an officer.

This action could prove to be fatal to the suspect when apprehended.

I remember the rage I felt at the time and knew that this suspect needed to end up in jail or a hospital or a morgue. Our San Jose citizens were mostly pro-police and felt the same way as I felt when one of our officers was hurt. Our image was very high with the public. One of the reasons I had transferred out of San Bernardino sheriff's department. I felt that I had left a good department in order to be hired on to a truly great department. Also, the pay was much better.

San Jose required all officers to have at least sixty units of college credits. Many officers had master's and doctor's degrees. Some had law degrees, and there were former airline pilots. One officer was a former major in the army, and another was a former captain and phantom pilot in Vietnam. These were truly professional people, and I was proud to work for one of the finest police departments.

I was driving my unmarked detective's car in the city and heard on the police radio that the suspect who was a passenger, Willy, had turned himself in at the corner of Blossom Hill and Almaden Road.

He did not want to be shot by angry police and was not the one who had tried to run the officer down. I arrived and saw that the suspect was already handcuffed in the back of a patrol car. I asked the officer if I could interview him, in which the officer agreed. I seated myself in the back seat with the suspect. I was not wearing my gun at the time and left it in my briefcase to avoid an officer safety issue. I interviewed with a soft approach to relax the suspect into talking with me rather than have him "lawyer up." I asked him where Tyrone was and told him that it would help Willy later in court to help police. William Jones stated that Tyrone was hiding at a girlfriend's apartment on Blossom Hill somewhere west of our location. He stated that Tyrone was planning to leave San Jose and had probably already left. I thanked him and began driving through every parking lot west of that location on Blossom Hill Rd. After several apartment building locations, I located a white Monte Carlo with a dark brown top. I drove by quickly, as I did not want to alert the suspect, and I probably looked like a life insurance agent driving to work. The first three digits of the license plate were 1DD.

I drove out of the apartment complex and requested for the beat sergeant to meet with me at Blossom Hill and Vine St. Sgt. Kirk met with me approximately four minutes later.

San Jose is the largest city in the Bay Area, even larger than San Francisco, with close to one million residents.

The city itself has different beats where there is one sergeant and several officers per beat.

I was presently in the Adam district or beat. The sergeant's call sign was 5 Adam 10. I knew of Sgt. Kirk recently coming out of the SWAT unit, so I knew he would want to handle the arrest in a highly tactical manner.

When he arrived, I informed him that the suspect's vehicle was parked in one of car ports, but I had driven out quickly to avoid having the suspect think that he was being watched.

The Sergeant requested for additional patrol units to meet and assist in the arrest.

Before I go on, I need to explain about the character of the man that we would take into custody.

First, he was indeed dangerous and would not hesitate to take an officer's life to avoid going to jail. This was a high-risk arrest.

Second, I was going to go home that same day. I did not want to be named after a freeway somewhere. The city was paying me a great salary to remain active and ready for duty, not in a hospital and not in a morgue.

Third, as a single father, I had to go home that night to be with my two sons and have dinner ready. So if anyone was going to lose, it was going to be Tyrone.

I couldn't care what the news or what the press would surmise.

I couldn't care what the NAACP thought. I owed my city, the tax payers the protection they deserved, and if Tyrone felt he hated me, too bad. Many people think that they would like to become police officers.

They feel that they would be friendlier or they could solve the problems with understanding and talking.

Maybe more community policing. But the bottom line was that Tyrone only would understand one reality: he would either submit to police or he would die. Parents, please teach your children to obey police even if they don't want to. It's actually a crime not to obey even if they don't think they have done anything wrong. If you're a single parent, then you better double the warning. If something happens and your grown adult is killed by police, you will wish that you taught him or her this valuable lesson. If you taught them to hate police and society because you feel life has been unfair to you or your family, think hard. I have met police while I was growing up that I thought were jerks, but I always obeyed. Later, if I needed to, I could make a complaint to internal affairs or file a lawsuit.

As an officer, I even filed a complaint with the FBI against a small unprofessional police department in a town I lived at. I obtained positive results and ended the "you're in our town "mentality." But this is how we live in a civilized society.

There are countries where the strongest rule—but not in the United States.

My bachelor's degree was in criminology, so I studied and tried to understand how a criminal mind works and also how I could survive and go home at the end of my shift.

To make a long story short, Tyrone was going to lose, and I was going to win. Some police officers claim that they have been active for thirty years and only pulled their guns a few times. Believe me. If you search out criminals, one will be pulling out his gun constantly. Or when they get a call for service, they drive slow to allow other units to arrive before them. These same officers are the ones to tell citizens that there is nothing they can do to help them when a problem occurs.

I approached the car port where Tyrone's car was parked. I stand at 5'9" and weigh approximately 165 pounds. so I'm not the most threatening person to begin with. I was wearing a windbreaker jacket with my walkie-talkie stuck to the rear of my waist band. My windbreaker jacket hid my Glock .40 caliber pistol. A black male came outside the apartment and saw me. I did not look at him and walked to the neighboring apartment room and knocked on the door so I would not give up my identity. I needed to buy time and observe the possible suspect. A woman answered the door, and I showed her my badge with my back covering the badge. In a low voice, I announced that I was an undercover San Jose detective who was observing the black male and was not ready to give him my identity. It worked, and she understood. I made small talk and observed the suspect until it looked like he was going to approach his vehicle to drive away.

At this time, I approached him and drew out my Glock. I yelled, "San Jose Police, on your stomach, on the ground now!"

Tyrone only had a second to respond, but he somehow knew he was about to get shot. I may have been 5'9" and 165 pounds, but to Tyrone, I was the bogeyman, and I had come to collect.

Tyrone fell right to his stomach, and I yelled at him to place both hands behind his back, which he gladly did. I announced that I had my gun pointed directly at his spinal column. By this time, the poor black man was screaming for his girlfriend. It's funny how a grown man can run down a police officer one day without blinking, and the next day, he's screaming for his mama when the bogeyman is standing over him. I told Tyrone that he was making me nervous because of his screaming, and I was afraid that I might pull the trigger in error. He immediately stopped. I told Tyrone that I was going to handcuff him with one hand and the other hand still had a gun pointed at his spinal column. If he so much as moved, I would be pulling the trigger, and before I hit the ground, he would be a paraplegic. I spoke in a low volume, much like a dentist when advising a patient when inserting a needle. Tyrone turned out to be a cooperative patient, and he was handcuffed without incident. Imagine if a citizen walking by had a phone with a camera.

It would be on the six o'clock news of a poor black man being harassed by police for no apparent reason. I stepped back and withdrew my walkie-talkie, referred to as a "handpack." I informed the patrol units to come in calmly as the suspect was 10-15, meaning in custody. I never saw a man so relieved to be safely helped into the back seat of a patrol car. He had said that the man with the gun had the "look of the devil" in his eye. I'm not sure if Tyrone later decided to read the Bible after that encounter with police or not. He sure seemed terrified when he was being driven away.

I had to explain to the former SWAT sergeant that I was not trying to act like a cowboy and I had meant to handle the situation tactfully. But everything went down too fast, and I didn't want him back in his car. If he had sped off, he could have killed a citizen in the process.

I couldn't live with that, but I would rather face a grand jury investigation of a shooting of a poor unarmed black man.

Incidentally, if an armed officer is struggling with an unarmed man, the unarmed man could soon become armed if he is winning the fight. I saw this happen once on Santa Clara St. The officer was shot with his own weapon directly in the face. I was not going to let that happen, and I think I got the message through to Tyrone. I hope that grand juries and the press take this into consideration when reviewing police shootings.

To this day, I'm not sure what had terrified Tyrone as it did. Even his girlfriend did not come out of her apartment to scream at me, which I found unusual. Sometimes, I think angels help police when they are in distress. Romans 13 in the Bible speaks of law enforcers as being appointed by God as is the president and leaders in government. If you do believe in the Bible, which I hope you do, give it a read.

A Los Angeles police deputy working in a remote section of Palmdale California reported taking an armed and dangerous suspect into custody alone. The suspect chose not to shoot the deputy and was taken into custody. The suspect was asked why he did not try to shoot the deputy. He responded, "I would have, but there were two large deputies with him, and I would have clearly lost." Records and the report indicated that the deputy had indeed been alone.

This event happened in 1993 in which I was about midway through my police career. I had started as a reserve deputy sheriff with Fresno sheriff's department. I was then hired by San Bernardino Sheriff as a regular full-time deputy. At thirty-one years old, I was hired by San Jose Police, where I stayed and retired in 2010. I will need to start from the very beginning. My story includes miracles which, I think, are heavenly sent and possible angel sightings.

CHAPTER 2

———◇◈◇———

College Days

From the beginning of my career, I wasn't sure what I would major in when I got to a community college.

All during high school, I was mostly involved in auto shops. As a teenager, I was only interested in cars.

I had my draft number, and I supposed that I would be sent off to Vietnam. Older friends were being drafted and sent to Germany or Alaska in order to do their two years without being sent to Vietnam.

I was planning on possibly going in and requesting a helicopter pilot training. If granted, I know where I would be sent. I was a senior in high school in 1973. As luck would have it, the draft ended.

The older males that I knew were coming home, and they felt as if two years had been stolen from them.

I asked what they would do now that they were back. They said they were going to attend college with their GI benefits. I have always been one for listening to the advice of older or more experienced people.

Why learn a lesson the hard way?

I enrolled in Mt. San Antonio College in the fall of 1973. I didn't know what I would major in, and I actually did not know anyone who had gone to college, so I was on my own. I took a class in aviation for basic ground school. I also took a class in police science. I, of course, took all of my requirement classes necessary to complete an associate degree in something. I just wasn't sure.

After the first year, I found myself finally majoring in police science. I wasn't sure if I wanted to be a police officer, but I thought I could decide after I had my two-year degree. After I graduated, I went to Fullerton State University for one semester. I was able to commute from my parent's home in West Covina.

I decided I would go after my bachelor degree in criminology. I was thinking of becoming a detective or an FBI agent. After one semester at Fullerton, I decided to attend Fresno State College as they had one of the best criminology departments in the state.

In 1976, I was attending Fresno state and enrolled in a reserve deputy class where you were actually sworn in as a reserve deputy. I could ride in a patrol car with a regular deputy one day of the week and wear a full uniform.

I was given a shooting course and firearms training, so I was carrying a 9mm Smith & Wesson Auto when riding on patrol. In addition, the reserves could work in the jail for $5.00 an hour, which was pretty good for 1976.

My very first shift in patrol was scheduled for a Saturday graveyard shift starting at eleven p.m.

Being in college, I was naturally attending college activities. That afternoon, I attended a concert in the outside grass area of Fresno State University. I remember drinking beer and having beer spilled on me.

I still wanted to enjoy college life at twenty-one years of age. I knew I had to get back to the dorms in order to shower and be sober from the concert. Papa Doo Run Run was playing and they sang all Beach Boy hits.

I remember climbing out of my car and walking into the Fresno sheriff's department for the first time in uniform.

My uniform was new and stiff and bright. My Sam Browne gun belt was stiff and shiny.

My baton seemed very long and kept hitting my knee as I walked. I felt like a fish out of water.

My whole attire screamed, "Look at the rookie!" I walked into the briefing room, and I could tell the deputies were thinking, *Another reserve. Hope he's not assigned to ride with me.* I walked to the desk where forms were kept and started collecting several of each form depending on the type of crime which would be reported that evening. A deputy stood beside me and said, "I see you're expecting a pretty busy night, huh?" Man, I felt stupid and awkward.

I was assigned to ride with a deputy named Craig. I explained to him, when we were loading up the patrol car, that this was my very first time in patrol. We had been trained to obey the deputy and ask what he expected on a car stop. Some deputies wanted the reserve to remain at the patrol car, and some did not mind the reserve approaching the violator's car. Craig appeared to be about thirty years old. He advised to stay by the patrol car. When the violator and situation appeared okay, I could approach and stand on the right side of the violator's car and look for any suspicious movement or substance.

As soon as our patrol car cleared the sheriff's station, a call came on that Fresno police were in pursuit of a vehicle traveling at a high rate down Shaw Ave. Craig immediately attached to the call, and off we sped, code 3 with lights and siren. Fresno can be a very violent town consisting of Mexican gangs of Norteños, Sureños, Mexican mafia—you name it. We drove up on the police vehicle and became a secondary in the pursuit. The suspect's car was an early 1960s Chevrolet Impala. The front wheel had apparently hit something, and the wheel was now bent in and scraping on the metal frame of the car. This was sending sparks shooting fifteen to twenty feet up in the air. We were basically pursuing a giant sparkler down a busy street in downtown Fresno. The violator turned onto a one-way street and was heading in the wrong direction of traffic! I saw headlights coming directly at us as cars dodged to avoid hitting the patrol cars. The violator turned right, and Craig immediately turned right through a parking lot to reduce distance. The violator crashed, and we skidded directly next to the violator.

My passenger door was five feet away from the suspect! I got out of the car without knowing whether to pull my gun out or not! I noticed Craig and the police officer had their guns out, so I figured I should probably pull mine too. Although we're trained in practical situations, it is completely different when everything is happening so fast.

I immediately ran to the back of the patrol car and positioned myself over the trunk lid with my weapon pointed at a young Hispanic man. The police officer had a shotgun in his hands and ordered the suspect out of the car. He instructed the suspect to place both hands on the back of his head with his fingers interlaced. The police officer yelled, "Take him, deputy!" I didn't realize he was speaking to me. He yelled again, "I said take him, deputy!" I realized he was speaking to me. Wow!

I wasn't ready for the world to explode so quickly all around me. After all, this was my first night.

Actually, my first hour!

I approached the suspect and holstered my gun. I grabbed my handcuffs, praying that my handcuffing training and technique would apply itself accordingly. The handcuffs came down on his right wrist.

I spun his wrist around and positioned it down to his lower back area. With my right hand, I held it stable, and with my left hand, I grabbed his left wrist and twisted in down to his lower back and snapped his wrist into the awaiting cuff—perfect! Finally, I did something right that evening.

The Fresno police officer approached and grabbed both of the suspect's wrists and lifted him and slammed his body into the hood of the suspect's car.

After a high-speed pursuit such as this, adrenalin flows, and tempers rise because of a dangerous situation.

Although police enter the occupation for the excitement, they still are emotional beings and subject to venting anger at the suspect that caused the situation.

I felt that the officer's actions were uncalled for, but I understood that he had gone through this ritual many times.

Earlier that day, I was a college student. This evening, I was now a law enforcement officer dedicated to arresting dangerous suspects who didn't care about my safety. I decided to shelve my opinion until I had more experience.

Don't judge a man until you've walked a mile in his shoes.

We got back into the patrol car and proceeded to our assigned beat. I remember thinking to myself, *This is going to be a long thirty-year career!*

While driving down the avenue, a lowered Chevy was approaching us with no headlights turned on. We swung a U-turn and flipped on the overhead lights with both spotlights on the driver. He pulled over and found him to have an active warrant for his arrest. We arrested him and transported him to the Fresno jail.

Upon entering the jail for the first time, I smelled the stench of wino, dirty socks, and stale air inside. Drunks were standing against the bars and staring with blurry eyes. There was yelling, swearing, and insulting.

I felt as if I had entered through the gates of hell.

Craig filled out all the necessary paperwork, and we met with the booking officer who processed the suspect.

We were then able to leave the jail and went over to the gun lockers and placed our guns back in our holsters and drove away.

The rest of the evening was uneventful. After three a.m., it really slowed down, and I found myself fighting to stay awake. I would learn that police work is both sheer terror and confusion accompanied by long stretches of boredom. There is no in between.

It was going to be a long career, but I would later learn that the people in uniform were actually called to perform such assignments. The Bible actually explains this, and I was unaware of this until several years into my career after working with a Christian detective. I'll talk about that experience later in the book.

My next patrol ride along was on the day shift. I was assigned to a large officer with a huge attitude problem toward the sheriff's department. He was kind of funny actually. I could tell the department was just tolerating him before they could fire him. I asked him about my role in a car stop situation. He announced, "Don't worry. We aren't pulling any cars over. That's a good way to get your head blown off!" He further announced, "You're kind of small. You're probably gonna get your ass kicked in."

After thirty-four years later, he would probably be surprised to find out that it never happened.

Guess you just can't tell by looking at someone.

In Fresno, if you have a problem deputy, they would put the deputy out in a sector somewhere, meaning "the boondocks." We never got one call during the entire day! If you ever meet an officer or deputy with an attitude problem in a rural area, don't say I didn't warn you. We visited truck stops, because he was going to become a truck driver after he was fired.

He explained that the pay was better, and it would be healthier because he'd be less stationary.

He could not understand why a Fresno state college student would want to become a law enforcement officer. Once again, he would be surprised to learn that I would one day retire, making a six-figure salary, along with excellent retirement and medical benefits.

After a boring morning, we drove into an incorporated area of Fresno. This area is enforced by Fresno police. The area was close to a truck stop and red-light district. The prostitutes were working the street in broad daylight. They didn't even run when they saw the patrol car. He stopped next to a prostitute, and the prostitute immediately handed him a health card. He seemed surprised, and she explained that it would show that she was recently checked and was disease-free. We drove up to a second prostitute, and he held his hand out the window.

The black woman said, "What you want?" The deputy said, "Let's see it!" "See what?" "Your health card." She said, "I ain't got no health card." The deputy said, "Then you shouldn't be working the streets with no health card." By the time our shift ended, I was practically hysterical from laughing so hard. This guy was unbelievable, and I certainly hope that Fresno sheriff did not waste any time firing him.

I graduated from Fresno University in 1977 with a bachelor's degree in criminology, and my next two departments would be working with officers and deputies who were far more professional than this guy. Cities and counties take note: "You get what you pay for." When a city pays a low wage, you won't get the cream of the crop, and you will be asking for a lot of lawsuits.

CHAPTER 3

———— ◈ ————

The Academy

After college, I went back to live with my parents in Southern California. I began signing up for different departments. While I was waiting at home, I got several side jobs. A person shouldn't sit around and wait for their dream job. *The dream job may never come*, as my dad had taught me. Learn different talents, but don't sit on your rear end and complain about being unemployed.

I obtained a job at tune-up masters for tuning up cars. After two months, I decided that this job wasn't for me. They phoned me at home and asked if I would stay on. They said they would send me to a lie detector machine training. I could then be able to interview employees in theft matters and still be a mechanic when needed. I thanked them for the opportunity but declined. I left this job in good standing in case I had to return. Always make yourself a good employee, and you'll always have someone who will hire you. You'll never have to say, "I can't find a job."

Work at McDonald's if you have to. Then find other jobs as people will notice you and want to employ you. I have met people who worked in various businesses that were a pleasure to meet and help me. They were grateful for their jobs and for their health. There were also others who were so miserable that I wasn't sure why they were there. Our Lord loves a grateful heart.

Don't just be grateful at Thanksgiving.

My next job was as a security guard. With my bachelor's degree, I walked around Kern's plant in Industry, California. One female security guard, standing at about five feet tall, looked up at me and said that she didn't think I was tall enough to be a police officer. I found that peculiar and told her that standing at her five-foot level and looking up at me, I thought that I would appear like a basketball player to her. Anyway, I could tell that this employee was a true career security officer with her intelligence that she was sharing with me.

I lasted about two months and then found another job as a private investigator. During this time, I was testing for various departments. I placed an application for a jailor job for El Monte police. The pay was horrible, but I wanted my foot in a door. They told me I was overeducated and did not receive a job interview.

As a private investigator, I found I was mostly following unfaithful spouses in my truck. I would have to wait for hours outside a home for a car to leave. Then I would tail the car to find out where it went. I was amazed to learn that my boss was collecting $300 an hour for this action, and it was the year 1977. I only stayed two weeks at this job, because in order to tail someone, you have to stay back and then blow through red lights to stay with the person. I could not afford this on my driving record if I wanted to later pass a background test for police employment.

I had placed a resume with Riverside police and received a notice for an oral interview after passing their written exam. When you go into an interview, you have to explain why you would want to work in the city of Riverside. All I could come up with was that it would be close to Big Bear and the mountain areas located in San Bernardino County. Wrong answer. They wanted to know why I was interested in Riverside, which I had not prepared a proper statement for. Oh, well.

Next, I drove up to Lake Tahoe and took their written exam. The department was small and had low pay. They explained that they would take the top five scores, and the candidates would receive an invitation to take the oral exam. I did not receive an invitation. By now, many people would be sitting in a bar and crying in their beer. No, keep trying. I remember getting on my knees and praying.

That's how bad I wanted the job. I told the Lord that I would always fulfill my duties in his name. After thirty-two years and retirement, I believe I fulfilled my promise.

When you go to test for a position like a deputy or officer, you better want it bad enough to taste it. You'll be competing with some of the best candidates that want it that bad.

Remember, they usually accept three candidates for every thousand applicants in California. Fifty percent get washed out by the back Xray alone. Always have a backup plan.

I took a written exam for San Bernardino sheriff's department and passed. I was then invited to take the oral exam. During my college days, I had taken a one-day course with Los Angeles police on tips for passing an oral exam. I was grateful for this preparation.

I was excited and told the interviewers why San Bernardino was the best department in the whole wide world. I could work in the city of San Bernardino or work at a substation in the desert area or the beautiful mountains of Big Bear. I could also remain working at the jail if I desired, and I let them know I had experience at Fresno jail. They loved my enthusiasm, or at least, I think they did they did, because I was selected to participate in the hiring interview. I was also placed on a treadmill, and my heart was monitored, along with a back Xray. I passed the eye exam, and on the day of weigh-in, I slouched down to become one inch shorter. I had drunk two malts and ate bananas to get my weight prepared for qualifying. The medical examiner said, "You barely made it." I would tell you my weight, but it was too embarrassing. At least the department would never have to worry about me being overweight in later years. I was only twenty-three years old at the time of my testing.

In my defense, I have to bring up the fact that the average Navy Seal as a special operator is 5'9", 160 pounds, and they are fierce and deadly.

My hiring interview was arranged, and I met with the under-sheriff. He was worried about my record of switching jobs so much after college. "You're just not serious enough. The academy is a high-stress academy, and my fear is that you will only last two days." I assured him that with my bachelor's degree in criminology, I was indeed serious. I then began to plead, "Sir, I can make it through the academy, but I can't prove it to you unless you open a door for me."

I remembered they like being called sir a lot. More points. "Please open this door and give me the opportunity to show you." After a moment, he responded, "Okay, but . . . I believe you will wash out in two days. And you better get that haircut!" I got up and stated, "Yes, sir. Thank you, sir."

Sure, I came close to crawling, but in the end, I got the job. At this point, the only way I was going to drop out of the academy was if they took me out on a stretcher.

I was immediately hired and put to work at their low security jail called Glen Helen. This is located a few miles from where the tragic San Bernardino terrorist shooting would later occur in 2015. The academy would start in a few months for me. The academy is located about one mile away. I really did not like working at Glen Helen, but that's the life of a San Bernardino deputy sheriff. In November of 1977, the academy would start on Monday. I had my uniform dry cleaned and most of my equipment cleaned. My gun belt was sprayed with high-gloss leather paint, and my shoes were spit shined. I got a very short haircut, which would have to be cut once a week.

Believe me, they check on Monday. I told the barber my situation, and he gave me a discount, as some weeks, he would only have to trim the sides to give a recently shaved appearance.

I showed up on Monday, and we lined up for inspection. To my horror, I noticed that everyone had a hat on but me. How could I have forgotten a hat? One guy forgot his dress shoes and had green sneakers on. I think several of the field training officers came out of the marines.

They were probably fired from the marines for being too mean. We were screamed at, and I was ordered to have a written memo by tomorrow to explain my forgetfulness involving my hat. We were put down for push-ups and then more push-ups. We were then run into a classroom where we were told we would run everywhere for the next fourteen weeks. We picked a class president who was a former Green Beret and could show us how to line up in formation and pivot when turning and also march in formation. From then on, we were screamed at when going on bathroom breaks and put down for more push-ups, sit-ups, and pull-ups.

At lunch, we would march to Glen Helen to eat where the inmates ate. The food was horrible at this place. You could burp one hour later and retaste the burger or macaroni. When typing a memo, it had to be at least one page long, and it had to have a 1 ½ inch margin on the right side and 1 ½ inch from the top. In the morning, they would measure with a ruler, and if it was off, you redo it with another one-page memo describing how you would not make another mistake. Imagine having to write one page on how you had forgotten to purchase a hat and the importance of having a hat. If you made a mistake, you could not use whiteout.

You had to retype the entire memo. They would hold your paperwork up to a light to identify if whiteout had been used. I tried to slip one in one time, but they located the whiteout correction. I then wrote it over that night with a one-page memo on why it would never happen again. In one day, you could get several memos and needed to be completed that night at home after a long day of running, push-ups, and being screamed at. One night, I was up until three a.m. I remember pulling my pillow apart in frustration. I then slept for two hours before getting up at five a.m.

On mornings, we had the first two hours of physical training, which I totally enjoyed. We would run up to ten miles without being yelled at. Our first week washed out several trainees. One guy was throwing up after running only one mile. Others were wearing arm slings and crutches.

One FTO screamed that we looked like patients in a hospital ward. I was glad to have prepared knowing that we would have physical challenges. The physical was not bad for me; it was the memos that I hated.

Most of my class of the 55th were deputies. We also trained Barstow police, Rialto police, San Bernardino police, Colton police. The deputies were abused more than the outside agencies.

Also, the deputies had to work an eight-hour shift on the weekend at Glen Helen. I hoped for a day shift or swing shift assignment, because a graveyard shift was a killer to stay awake.

For fourteen weeks, I had entered into hell.

The FTOs would check everyone's car during class to see if it was locked, because our guns and equipment were inside. One day, a deputy did not lock his car. The FTOs called us into immediate formation. They told us a false story about two inmates escaping from Glen Helen.

They said one inmate was seen with a gun. We were ordered to go to our cars and immediately put on our duty belts with guns and batons as we were going after the escapees. We were ordered into formation, and one deputy did not have a gun in his holster. He was immediately screamed at, "Ramsey, where is your gun?" "Sir, I don't know, sir!" We were ordered into the class. The FTO then announced that two detectives stopped the fleeing suspects near the freeway, and they were in custody. "The gun was recovered," they explained. The FTO stood by the chalkboard with the chalk, ready to write. "Ramsey, what's the serial number of your gun. We'll find out if it's the same one as what the inmates had." "Sir, I can't remember." "Ramsey, I want your badge on my desk in the morning!" By this time, Ramsey was completely white as a ghost.

Later, we learned that the escape was all staged, and the FTO had Ramsey's gun in his office.

Ramsey was never fired, but he probably aged several years after that and always checked his car to see if it was locked. This was indeed a true stress academy. There had been a Marine in the class ahead of us. I asked him if Marine boot camp was as hard. He said that the physical was harder in the Marines, but the mind games were worst here at the sheriff's academy, along with the stress.

As I mentioned earlier, when assigned to writing a memo, it had to be one page long. If you had a thread on your uniform and assigned a memo, you had to type for one page about the importance of not having any more threads or lint on your uniform. It required imagination to come up with a story about thread.

We received training in pursuit driving from the CHP, California Highway Patrol. We had to drive on a skid pan, which was asphalt with a sprinkler system to keep it wet. The tires on the car were bald so the car would be able to go into an uncontrollable skid. You would then attempt to pull the car out of the skid. We wore helmets, and the cars had roll bars inside. My nemesis and worst FTO climbed into the passenger seat and warned me not to roll the car. I put it into a minor side skid and pulled out. He screamed at me to drive in a manner that would not put him to sleep. I then got my speed up and put it into a terrifying two-car spin then corrected the spin. The FTO seemed pleased and came close to smiling.

Back in the classroom, the CHP instructor sent us out for a bathroom break. The FTO came out and screamed and had us get down and do fifty push-ups. Then sit-ups and ordered us back into the classroom. My hands were dirty because of asphalt. The CHP apologized for letting us out for the break. He disagreed with the way we were being treated. He explained that at the CHP academy, they were treated like adults. But this was a true stress academy.

The FBI then came for a few weeks and taught us shooting, which I enjoyed. We were told prior to dry fire our guns empty every night, fifty times to work the stiff revolvers in and to build a callus on our trigger finger. We shot one thousand five hundred rounds a day. The heat of the revolver would burn you if you touched the cylinder. These were .357 caliber revolvers with hollow point bullets. After a couple weeks, we had fired thousands of rounds. Our shoulders were sore from the numerous shotgun blasts, and we went home with bruises to prove it.

Towards the final few weeks of the academy, the FTOs started to ignore us, and we were begging to be put down for push-ups. My arms no longer screamed with pain, and sit-ups no longer hurt. We watched an FTO sitting at his desk, correcting papers. We dropped our batons on the ground so we could be screamed at, but he yawned and ignored us. Our president then ordered us down for push-ups. The FTO finally came out and ordered us in the classroom.

One of the last weeks of class, we had the SWAT team give a course. While on break, they maced the floor between our desks. We sat in class while they instructed, and our eyes were burning, and I could not open my eyes. After minutes, an FTO came in and screamed that we were a bunch of crybabies and told us to go into the bathroom to rinse our eyes. I made my way outside, feeling for the wall and the direction of the bathroom. I cracked my eyes open once to get the direction memorized then headed in the proper direction. Once inside the restroom, there were only four or five sinks. Thirty recruits then took turns rinsing and letting the person behind him rinse after only a few seconds. One recruit went to the toilet bowl to rinse so he could take his time rinsing.

This was 1978, and most of the practices are no longer done due to lawsuits. We could not wait for graduation day. Our families and girlfriends were invited for the ceremony. We had received a delicious prime dinner at Glen Helen. The sheriff flew in a Huey helicopter and landed next to the ceremony—quite impressive. I had survived!

The celebration was at the Disney Hotel. My girlfriend at the time had accompanied me.

The FBI and CHP instructors also were invited. We had gotten our orders. Deputies who put in for substations, such as Needles on the Colorado River, did not have to work the jail or Glen Helen and went directly to patrol. I received orders for the main jail, where I would be there for about eleven months. I was glad to not have to work at Glen Helen again.

CHAPTER 4

―――――◇◆◇――――――

Main Jail

As I had stated, I was glad I did not have to go back to Glen Helen, the minimum security jail.

The main jail was the next step up. I had been told that I would have to share a locker with another deputy. My first day found me with a slight touch of the flu. I opened the locker and saw that the other deputy had not cleared out half of the locker for me. I merely pushed his hangers to one side to make room for my clothing. I began working on the second floor where I would have to operate doors to let inmates out into a long corridor. The inmates could then walk down a hallway where they would have to walk single file with their hands in their pockets at all times. A deputy in an enclosed guard shack could watch the procedure and call out on the phone system if a fight broke out. The inmates were then ushered in the mess hall, where they would remain in single file to grab their trays and walk through a cafeteria-type line to obtain their food. They were not allowed to talk during the whole lunch time process. There could be about eighty to one hundred inmates eating and only three deputies supervising. If a fight broke out, you had to escort the violator out. If a riot broke out, it would be best to head for the exit where the doors would be locked down. It's a scary feeling at first, and I'm glad I never had to go through a jail riot. When done, the inmates were excused one table at a time to return to their cells, which usually housed four inmates per cell.

Halfway through my shift, I heard a deputy yelling my last name, "Orok! Where's Orok?" My name is pronounced Or-Rock. I was met with a hotheaded deputy who wanted to know why I moved his clothing over in his locker. I told him that his locker should have been ready and half vacant for my belongings. He seemed to cool off somewhat and said that no one had told him he would be sharing his locker with someone. I explained that I was assigned to half the locker and had nowhere else to store my clothing. I later learned that he had been a street deputy for a while, and he was too much of an "edge" and could not cope with the uncertainty of the street and had to come back to the jail. He was also a black belt in karate with a volatile temper. He was further in the transportation unit of inmates to court hearings. Whenever you see sheriff's buses and vans, they are transporting to or from court houses. The deputies are known for screaming at jailors for doors to be opened and immediately to have inmates ready for transport. Basically, they have big mouths and think they own the jail. On the other hand, they have to put up with judges and attorneys who want their clients on time for court, so they are under a lot of stress. Anyway, the deputy and I came to an understanding, and we got along well after that. This deputy left law enforcement about a year later. The job's not for everybody.

The great thing about being a deputy is that you get to live part-time in jail with people that are criminals who you will later be arresting. You know how they think, and they will try to con you. You learn to use a controlling voice and know how to fight if necessary. I think you learn how to read them.

If a deputy wanted to get in a lot of fights, then he would work in central booking. Here is where the inmate is first brought in and fingerprinted and searched. The drunks would often times want to fight and not submit to being fingerprinted. The inmate would then be taken to an isolation cell to wait for the next shift to process him. Once sober, the inmate was entirely different, and some were even pretty nice guys. Alcohol makes some people quite obnoxious and belligerent.

On one evening, I was working on second floor. One large belligerent inmate began yelling at me when I gave him an order.

He approached me, and I hit him in the face as the fight was on. A "trusty" inmate ran to the guard shack to report a deputy being assaulted in a fight. I got one arm behind his back and rammed his head into a metal door. I thought he would use his other free hand to cushion his impact, but he didn't. His head went right into the door. Other deputies arrived, and he was fully handcuffed. He eye was fully swollen shut and swelled. I then looked at my right hand and saw that my knuckle on my smallest finger was dislocated about half an inch up from its normal position. I was sent to the hospital where I learned I had what's called a boxer's fracture, and my right hand would be in a cast for about a month.

I can't describe how much I missed the use of my prominent hand. Going to the bathroom and then wiping myself with my off-hand was extremely difficult. Something you never think about. Never hit someone in the head. Their head is harder than one's fist. If you have to do a survival move, hit him in the throat. Lesson learned. I learned more about actual fighting in the jail than in all my self-defense classes in college and the academy. I learned what worked for me and what didn't. I'm not a big believer in karate students, because they don't actually get into fights in a jail or bar. They have a false sense of security. I have never seen a karate black belt beat up police or inmates. The few that have taken a fighting stance got punched out or choked out.

Our bodies are a miraculous, sensitive, intricate machine. Lose one small part, and you will see how much it functioned and how much you miss it. I had to learn to write with my left hand.

Why did I have to hit that guy in the head? I could have kicked him. I thought to myself, *Oh, no, not another life lesson.*

When working in jail or a law enforcement environment, you have to take control in situations.

When someone gets aggressive, you have to get more aggressive. The average person doesn't understand this. That's why the iPhone with the camera is so effective in showing an aggressive officer but fails to show the earlier actions of the suspect's aggression toward the officer. One merely shows a one-sided view to the media.

When I was twenty years old, I was in altercation with a guy that I grew up with and had a disagreement.

The person was two years older and could be a huge bully if he didn't get his way. I now believe he was bipolar and psychotic but not at the time. He had dropped out of high school and was drafted into the Army. In the Army boot camp, he was kicked out, probably for being nuts. He received an honorable discharge, which includes government benefits. He was basically a loser who never served our country but would receive a government check for life. Anyway, he threatened to beat my ass and rushed me. I thought it would turn into a wrestling match with other friends pulling us apart. Instead, he got me into a headlock then proceeded to smash my face with a fist and probably had large rings on. He also outweighed me by at least thirty pounds. This so-called childhood friend was basically trying to pulverize my face. I worked my way out of the headlock and came up with a mighty punch directly under his chin. I thought the hit would knock him out as he stumbled backward. His younger brother then jumped in between us and pushed me back, not wanting to control his brother. What a coward. I then noticed that the front of my T-shirt was bloody.

I received a large laceration on my forehead that could have used stitches, which I declined, and had two blackened eyes. This fight had changed my entire perception on being attacked by anyone.

After this incident, if anyone ever attempted to injure me, I would attack with any resource that was available to me. I learned more on that day than any other time in violent situations with nut cases. I believe that this way of thinking may have saved my life in lots of law enforcement situations. Unfortunately, I think some police officers learn this rule too late, resulting in injury or even death while on duty.

While growing up, I also lived two houses away from another nut case, also one year older than me. I remember once, he had gotten angry at me and got me on my back, and as he sat on my chest, he punched at my face. I remember my head bouncing off the payment on each blow until he was relieved of his tantrum.

Before this nut case was eighteen years old, he had gotten into a road rage incident with another driver. The other driver got out of his car with a crowbar and hit him on the head. My friend then stabbed the driver with a butcher knife. Both were arrested, and my friend was given a choice to go to juvenile hall or enlist in the armed service. He chose the Navy, and I believe he may not even be alive at the time of writing this book.

You see, I grew up with violent nut cases. That's why I think I felt so comfortable in both the jail and in law enforcement. I think God was preparing me for the occupation of deputy and police officer and detective. I truly understood the criminal mind and the selfish violent behavior. I feel deeply for the victim of assault and domestic violence. I understood that some people were better off in jail or the morgue if necessary. I also want to mention the fact that the people I mention do little for society but become a burden.

It costs $55,000 a year to keep an inmate in custody. Many are proud and even brag about the numerous prisons they've been sentenced to. They mark themselves with tattoos and display them proudly when on parole out in public. Lawyers have made jail comfortable for these individuals with three meals a day, color TV, and a warm bed. But in the end, every knee will bow before the King of Kings, and they will give account for their lives and their injury of innocent victims. I truly believe that God sees everything we do in this life, and that has been what has kept me an honest cop during my career. I've been far from perfect, but in order to survive law enforcement, you have to be honest. The longest I believe a bad cop can survive is five years—tops. He will eventually get caught. The bad cop will have to be placed in protective custody from other inmates, who will kill him if allowed. He is a disgrace to his family and his community.

In the Bible, look up Romans 13 and see the importance that God places on people of authority. They're assigned with a high expectation. Bill Clinton would not have passed a background test for a police officer position, yet at one time, he was the leader of the United States!

San Bernardino deputies put in about one year on average, until they were transferred out of the jail and assigned to a patrol assignment. Los Angeles deputies had to do about five years in jail before transferring to patrol stations. I had placed a request to transfer to Big Bear substation located in the pine trees of the mountain resort. Being a prime substation, I had about five years to wait.

During this time, my relationship with my girlfriend of four years had ended. What was worse was that I was working on the graveyard shift with zero dating social life. Why couldn't I be a "love 'em and leave 'em" type of guy? I was heartbroken and lonely. I needed to get out of the jail and could not wait for Big Bear. I placed a request for Victorville, a desert substation, and Fontana, a suburb of San Bernardino. Wherever I ended up would be fine with me. Also, I wasn't a Christian at the time, so I had no one to talk with and no one to pray to. I always believed in God. I just didn't have a personal relationship where I could pray and ask him what I should do. That would come later in life, several years later.

We had our own mailboxes located in a hallway. They were open boxes where anyone could see if you had a letter awaiting. The orders for transfer were always in a distinctive envelope. Deputies were getting orders for Rancho Cucamonga, Central San Bernardino, Barstow, 29 Palms, and even the Colorado River substations. One day, I saw the letter waiting in my box. The letter would determine where I would be living. Here goes. I opened the letter and read "Victorville." I would be living in the high desert, which is a busy substation. It was on the backside of Big Bear. I could drive up the backside of the mountain in forty-five minutes with no traffic. And get out of the snow easily when I wanted to. Also, deputies were known to conduct a variety of investigations and patrol and were known to promote easily from these busy substations. I would be in Victorville for the next seven years. I had been in the main jail for about thirteen months. I was ready for patrol duty. Same uniform, but now I would wear a bulletproof vest under my shirt and a gun belt.

CHAPTER 5

Victorville Substation

Climbing the Cajon Pass on Interstate 15 was a steep, windy drive. The smoggy San Bernardino Valley rose up to clean blue skies. Because it was December, the air was crisp and cold and made one feel alive with excitement. The confinement of a crowded city below gave way to an open, relaxed feeling with a bluer than blue sky. Out of all of the different climates I had worked or lived in, I enjoyed the high desert the most. Fresno was the worst, with thick, cold ground fog in the winter and muggy heat in the summer. The sky always had a tan haze to it. The high desert had a dry heat in the summer and was actually more comfortable than Fresno. But the skies were always blue. The afternoon wind could be annoying, but at night, the winds usually ceased. A night in the summer was very pleasant, and a million stars would come out. There is a saying that in the summer, nighttime is the desert's way of apologizing for the daytime.

A few weeks before moving, I made contact at the Victorville substation and met with the captain and the lieutenant. The lieutenant said that I would be with a training deputy for only a few days and then would need to immediately man a car by myself in order to handle calls. I would soon know how shorthanded the county was.

The first few days, I was on dayshift with Deputy Shree. He was an easygoing guy. From the Victorville station, we drove out seven miles to the unincorporated town of Hesperia. This was a town of

36

about thirty thousand people. We only had one other patrol car to help with calls or if we needed a backup. Day shift was uneventful, and I noticed that we went to a lot of report calls of burglary, theft, trespassing, illegal shooting on private property, and motorcycle dirt bike riding.

I remember renting my condo-type residence in Apple Valley. It was a brand-new unit with the smell of new carpeting and beautiful walnut cabinets. I was located only a few miles from the famous Roy Rogers residence, situated right on Hwy 18. I was amazed at his simple lifestyle, which was an ordinary house with an old Chevy pickup truck parked in front. Later, his son would build him a more elegant gated home on the Apple Valley golf course. I would even get to make an arrest on his driveway and meet with him in person.

Driving to the substation was only an eight-mile journey with no traffic. I really fell in love with the desert. In a few training days, I was in a patrol car alone for the first time in my life. I remember collecting as many different forms as I felt I needed. I found out that I was indeed a rolling secretary, going from one report call to the next.

I had a residential burglary, and I had to establish a point of entry. Then I located shoe tracks, which I had to sketch and measure. Then I got my camera and camera holder with shields. When taking a shoe track, the holder would flash the picture at an oblique angle to show a detailed photo of the ridges in the sole and could even make out distortions, such as in the case of one stepping on a nail, indicating a cut in the sole. Later, when a suspect was arrested, his shoes were taken for evidence, and in court, the photo could be enlarged to five feet in order to show the jury that the suspect's shoes positively matched the prints from the crime scene. Crooks were always careful about fingerprints and gave no regard to their foot tracks when committing burglaries. I could tell how many suspects were involved and later learned to track suspects for miles. The look on their face was to die for when I apprehended them a few miles away. It was just like on television in Westerns when an Indian tracker would track for the army.

I had to write down information for the report and items taken. Then came fingerprinting, which I hated. I had to sprinkle graphite dust onto a possible location. The dust was filthy, and I would get it on my hands and breathe it up my nose. When I got a visible or latent print, I would get tape out and prepare to then transfer the latent onto a three by five fingerprint card. I usually didn't get prints, because even when a crook forgot gloves, he would take his socks off and place them over his hands. Once the call was completed, I would drive down the street to begin writing several pages of report.

Usually, the dispatcher would figure out I spent enough time at a call and would check my progress before giving me another burglary call. The former report would have to be done at the end of my shift for overtime pay. Then I would get a "theft of gas" call from a car then possibly illegal dirt bike riders on private property. Day shift was nonstop report writing calls. I was lucky if there was another deputy to help with the calls. Some days I was alone to answer calls in a town of thirty thousand people.

Day shift was not a fun time to be a deputy. Although I did gain a lot of valuable experience in investigating and court testimony. Every two months, we would switch from day shift to graveyard, and two months later, you would change to swing shift—my favorite shift. You were allowed to change shifts if another deputy wanted to change. Some worked mainly graveyard to avoid the tremendous amount of reports and paperwork. The heat was horrible in the summertime, with bad working air conditioners that were more like fans. If you stayed at idle to write a report, the car would overheat.

The bulletproof vest I wore under my shirt made my agony worse. At end of shift, my undershirt was soaked, and my vest smelled and had to be hung outside in order to dry for the following day.

My first solo arrest was Christmas day 1980-12-25. A Union 76 gas station on Bear Valley Road reported that an intoxicated woman had just driven away from the station, westbound on Bear Valley Road.

I arrived several minutes later and listened to the attendant. I felt that she was long gone, but the attendant said that the driver was driving very slowly. I accelerated fully westbound on the highway, listening to the four barrels opening on the carburetor. Near the High Desert College, I located the car and affected a vehicle stop.

I got the woman out and saw that she had trouble standing. I was relieved that I did not have to conduct a sobriety test, because I had never done one, and I was afraid as a rookie doing a false arrest on my first customer of my career. I booked her into the Victorville jail and wished her a Merry Christmas as I cleared to go back into service and complete my report. My very first solo arrest and I was truly honored to place her into custody before she killed somebody.

In a few months, I was transferred to the graveyard shift. I was so relieved to get away from the constant report writing calls. I actually got to enjoy free patrol driving where I could hunt something down and make an arrest. There were a lot of prowler calls but were usually just noises that made people uneasy, usually the wind or a house cat prowling around. When getting out of the car, I would pull up slowly with my lights off. I would shut my car door quietly and walk slowly up and observe any noises or movement. I used to walk around with my flashlight off until one particular night. I had come around the backyard, and I immediately felt cobwebs. I turned on my flashlight and saw several huge black widows hanging on the cobweb. I almost walked into them, and I noted that black widows are huge in the desert. I then learned to just use discretion, whether I used my flashlight or not.

One night, I got a prowler call from a house located on a hill away from other houses. I first made contact at the front door and met with an old woman with long flowing grey hair which was cascading down her back. She looked as if she might have ridden a broomstick when her car was down for repairs. She advised that a noise came from the rear yard. I slowly made my way around the backyard in the dark. When I got next to a darkened window, the drapes suddenly were ripped back, and there in the window was a face glaring at me. I came close to withdrawing my .357 magnum and ventilating the figure, when it dawned on me that it was the woman. Why couldn't she just crack the curtain and peak out like a normal person does? Anyway, I found no one in the backyard, and I cleared the call before I found myself floating in a boiling pot of water or, worse, had her put a spell on me. She probably never saw a patrol drive away as fast as I did that night as my car kicked up dust on the dirt road. Just kidding. I would go back if necessary, but it was spooky!

Several weeks later, I would get another call in the area. The neighbors reported that a man living alone had not been seen outside in a while. His car was still outside, and there were newspapers in driveway. I made contact and noted weeks of mail in the mailbox. I rang the doorbell of the darkened house. With no answer, I walked around the darkened house and noted bugs on the window screens.

I then smelled the odor of rotting flesh and knew what awaited me inside the home. I would need to remove the screen and slide the window open and crawl inside. I remember my recent encounter with the "witch lady," and I was in no mood to go through that ordeal again. At least, not alone. I needed at least one witness to tell the story of my demise to my relatives. I radioed dispatch for another unit to assist me. The deputy came from several miles away. I explained to the deputy that I would need to go into the house and find the body. But there was no way I was going into that spooky house alone. He fully understood and agreed to wait by the back door until I could crawl through the window and unlock the back door. Believe me, when I landed on the kitchen floor, it seemed like a long way to the back door before I could unlock it. We then started switching on lights until I was in the master bedroom and found the deceased lying on the floor. Because of the decay and time of death, the victim was blackened and swelled to appear as if he were three hundred fifty pounds. With all the lights on, I thanked the deputy and waved him off. I had dispatch phone the coroner and with an ETA of forty-minutes minutes. I decided to wait outside to begin my report. When the coroner arrived, he immediately put a dab of Vicks rub inside his nostrils. He offered me some, and it did, in fact, help with the smell of the decaying body.

I would become quite familiar with the coroner on many more dead body calls in the desert.

*****

On a dayshift call, I got a call of a dead body near the railroad tracks down a canyon by the Mojave Narrows. I hiked down into the canyon and saw the upper torso of a young woman. She still held onto her purse with one hand. Her body was severed in two. Her lower half of her body was several feet away. It appeared as if her body had been cut in two by a guillotine. The torso had separated and sealed so there was not a lot of blood coming out. I notified the coroner with his team to remove the two body halves. It appeared that the young woman had tried to jump on the train but was unsuccessful. The lower half of her body had swung under the train, and the wheels cut her in half like a razor blade.

*****

During my time so far, I had witnessed quite a few dead bodies and accidents. My faith in God was not very strong at this time. I stilled believed, but I had too many questions and no one to talk to about God. I did not attend church at this time.

My social life was terrible, and my dating life consisted of going out with females that I would meet at restaurants, hospitals, etc. I tried the night club scene for about four months. I found that night clubs or bars had the loneliest, sad-storied, lost people of all. These consisted of "cry in your beer" type sad people. Basically, my social life was horrible. There was no hope or light in this area of my life.

I did meet a woman who was attractive and working as a blood tech at Victorville Hospital. She didn't like drinking and spoke of waiting for marriage for any sexual experiences. She explained that she was a Christian, and I attended a church service with her at a Baptist Church. I hadn't realized this at the time, but God was trying to show me the way. I would later get married in this same church to another woman, and I would begin to follow the Lord in a very shallow way. It wasn't good, but at least it was a start. My eldest son would attend this same church about thirty years later. Talk about coincidence, but these miracles are happening around us all the time with God talking to us.

The problem is that we're too thickheaded or dense to hear his voice. We keep walking down dead-end roads and making the same stupid mistakes. Believe me; I was very successful in my career but completely stupid at the dating scene. I would, many years later, learn to talk with Jesus as my friend and read my Bible. All the answers were there in the Bible. I was an excellent investigator but couldn't learn how to solve the road map to life. To this day, I am grateful for dating this Christian woman and for her showing me the light even if we never got into a serious relationship.

Our world consists of the world we experience every day, but there is also a supernatural realm as well.

Even if you don't believe it, it still exists. We will be in the physical world on average about seventy-five years.

But the supernatural world will last forever. If you are smart enough to believe in God, you also have to believe in his angels. If you believe in angels, you also have to believe in demons. You have to believe in a force out there trying to destroy you, and I don't just mean criminals. I have seen more officers kill themselves with their own guns rather than a criminal killing them. Someone is talking to them, but they refuse to believe in demons. I have been in almost every bad experience that these officers have been in, and I have served far longer and never thought of suicide. I don't credit myself, but my Savior has protected me. I'm no match for a demon speaking lies to me, but they tremble when I mention who my backup is Jesus. If you want to see more officers who don't believe, just pick up a newspaper and read about officers arrested for drug usage, stealing, lying in court, shooting an unarmed person running from them, affairs with women while they are still married, alcohol problems. The list goes on and on, and all of them think belief in God is silly. Really!

Even a drug addict has got to believe in a higher power in order to rid themselves of life-threatening addictions that make them a slave from something that is destroying themselves. There is a hidden criminal out there destroying police officers, and it lies in the supernatural realm.

As Captain Barbossa stated to Elizabeth in *Pirates of the Caribbean*, "You best start believing in ghost stories. You're in one!" Actually, there is a demonic spiritual world out there, and it waits like a lion to devour and destroy you. You better have backup!

CHAPTER 6

———◆◈◆———

Victorville Substation Jail

Victorville had a small temporary subjail capable of holding up to seventy inmates. This jail served to hold inmates for court and also on weekends, until the inmates could be transported back to San Bernardino main jail. Occasionally, I would come to work expecting to climb into a patrol car, only to learn that I would need to work the jail. Bummer. While working the jail, you would need to conduct a head count of inmates before relieving the former shift's deputy. You would be expected to book and process any incoming arrests from deputies or CHP officers and babysit the existing inmates who would whine for showers, phone calls, or day room privileges. In addition, there were three inmate workers known as "trusties" who would cook, gas patrol cars, or any other type of manual work needed.

I learned early while working the main jail that these were all human beings who liked to be treated fairly, which I did. Other deputies could care less. The inmates would yell all shift long or get into fights in order to make the deputies' job tougher. The cells contained four beds each. There was one hall that contained single-man units. There was a small kitchen where a trusty would heat TV dinners for the inmates and could cook a meal for the trusty and deputy. The first thing I would do is inform the four-man units that the when their doors would open, they were to step outside and walk down a secured hallway to the dayroom. I would then lock the dayroom and cell doors and check to see that no one stayed behind in the cells.

I then informed the inmates that I wanted everyone to take their showers that were located in the day room, and they gladly agreed. I informed them that I would grant three people five-minute phone calls. They were left to decide who needed the phone calls the most. I would return in a few minutes to let the three out and use the phone. After that, I wanted to hear no one yell for a phone call. I advised them that the trusty would place a bucket and mop in the day room for them to clean. If they cleaned, they would be allowed coffee and TV privileges until my shift was over. If there were any fights, everyone would return for lockdown.

I let them know that I didn't want to be there as much as they didn't want to be there. But we were going to make it as pleasant as possible. I never had a problem in the jail with inmates.

Next, I would talk to the cook trusty and asked if he liked cooking as his job. I didn't want anyone cooking who was not good at it. One time, I asked, and he said he preferred to be the gas attendant.

The gas attendant said he liked cooking, so I switched both their jobs. That evening, we enjoyed a delightful jail meal. Everyone was happy with my leadership in running this jail. I was then able to concentrate on booking and fingerprinting incoming arrests. I hated working this jail but made the best out of it. I was glad to have a job and glad to be a deputy.

I also got into trouble working this jail. I had booked a new arrest into custody and placed $600.00 of his property into a locker. A day later, when he was released, the money was missing. An investigation began involving me and the deputy that released him. We did not have a strong police union at the time, so we were basically thrown under the bus. I could not remember the number of the locker I placed the money in. I don't believe the other deputy took it. I think what happened is that when the release deputy released several inmates at one time, the wrong inmate received the $600.00 dollars and didn't speak up. Shocking!

We were just forming an internal affairs unit, and there was a hypnotist in the unit who could try to see if I could remember what locker number I had placed the money in. The lieutenant who didn't like me suggested that I should go down voluntary to San Bernardino to be hypnotized.

I wanted to get him off my back, and I was frankly curious and did not really believe in hypnosis.

I arrived and met with an attractive female who said she was a psychiatric counselor as well. I was expecting her to take out a pocket watch and start swinging it in front of me. Instead, she told me to concentrate looking at a fixture in the room, which I did. She spoke calmly and told me to close my eyes. I remember thinking that this wasn't going to work because of my strong mind. She explained that she was tying a string which held an inflatable balloon to a wrist. I felt the string on my wrist. She said the balloon would start raising my arm. Knowing that I wasn't hypnotized, I figured we would soon be done. To my amazement, my traitorous arm started to rise. She then told me that she would untie the balloon, and I could lower my arm. She then asked me what locker number I had placed the money in. I then began to laugh hysterically and couldn't stop. I felt like a little kid in the principal's office, and this made me laugh harder. I couldn't stop, and I kept telling myself that I would soon be fired when this was over.

She asked me another question, and this seemed even funnier. I had no control!

She advised me that I could now come out of my hypnotized state. I immediately began to earnestly apologize for my rudeness and asked her to forgive me. She immediately told me not to worry and that the investigators had stressed me to the point that I would never remember the locker number.

She said that I was interviewed improperly by the lieutenant and was treated like a suspect and her report would go to the sheriff. Seems the butt-kissing lieutenant was now in trouble. The other deputy refused the hypnosis, and so the lieutenant reasoned that the suspicion would focus on him.

CHAPTER 7

Miracles

It had been a beautiful weekend up in the high desert. It was Sunday, and the late afternoon would later surrender to a calm desert evening. A group of Christian teens from a church had spent the weekend at a Christian retreat in the pine forests of Big Bear Lake. The church bus had reliably arrived at the retreat. The teens had spent the weekend in deep devotion to God. They could have spent their time at home partying or just being lazy. But they had chosen to serve God in prayer and study the Bible. The bus was returning home and traveling down the backside of Big Bear, traveling down a steep, windy two-lane roadway. The bus driver kept pumping the brakes to slow the bus down. On a regular shoe, hydraulic brakes are helpful for the avoidance of overheating the brakes. But this was different; the brakes were air brakes. Pumping air brakes could result in braking failure.

When the bus was on the very last curve, the brakes failed. The bus ran off the roadway and into a canyon, overturning. The teens were severely injured. What had been a great weekend was now a nightmare. Paramedics and medical transports were summoned, and they were taken to several hospitals.

This was probably one of the times I was angry at God. Imagine, they came to worship and serve him, and he can't at least see them home safely! It was the very last curve, and the great God could not or would not keep them safe. I remember thinking, *Maybe God doesn't exist.*

If he does, maybe he just doesn't care. Either way, I was quite angry with him. I remember telling him, "I don't want to hate you, so maybe it's better that I say goodbye to you so I don't have to store up hate for you. Goodbye and don't let the door hit you on the way out."

I remember traveling down to the San Bernardino shopping mall and walking through stores. I would sometimes do that on my day off if I was depressed. My social life was gone, so I needed something to pass the time. I walked by a Barnes & Noble bookstore and looked through the magazines. Upon exiting, I glanced at the number one book section and the hot sellers. There was a book that caught my eye: *When Bad Things Happen to Good People*. Wow, how appropriate. I decided to buy the book. God has different ways of talking to people. I would later learn that God was trying to talk to me, and he often times used this method of getting my attention. Imagine, the creator of the universe wanted to take time out of his busy schedule to converse with me!

I bought the book and drove home. The author is a rabbi who wanted to try to explain the tragedies of the world to hurt and angry people. The author explained that he had a son who was born with a disease that would take his life sometime in his teens and that he, in fact, died.

The author explained that we live in a physical world with the consequences such as gravity and centrifugal forces constantly at work. Diseases were a reality in a fallen, sinful world with death affecting both good people as well as bad. Gravity and centrifugal force had propelled the church bus off the highway and also error on the driver's part. Okay, but I needed to see a miracle from a great God and not excuses. A few days later, I read about the collision in the high desert newspaper.

It just so happens that there were three helicopters in the area of the collision at the time. This was highly unusual. These helicopters were used for medevacs to hospitals. The men coordinating the air traffic did an admirable job directing the helicopters. Also, medical staff said that it was highly unusual that on a Sunday afternoon, all of the doctors were able to be contacted to report to three different hospitals in the area. Also, God didn't kill me for calling him a coward and nonloving God.

There were miracles happening, but I just could not identify them at the time. Also, God loved me and understood my anger, much like a father still loves a child even after the child shouts, "I hate you!" So good news, I was speaking to God again.

My Christian walk was still very shallow at this time in my life, but I was slowly learning. God probably thought I was a special education student who just needed extra loving.

I would see other miracles occur as well. While on a graveyard shift, I got a call to a suspicious circumstance to the rear of the old Roy Rogers Museum on Hwy 18 in Apple Valley. I arrived and noticed that a car had driven through a chain-linked fence. When the fence was struck, the upper tubular pipe of the fence had snapped but then came wiping through the windshield like a venomous snake attacking its victim. The two-inch pipeline drove directly through windshield and then through the driver's chest and came out the other side of the driver's chest and stopped at the seat. It looked like a scene out of *Alien*. To make matters even more gruesome, the driver was conscious and looking at me and groaning. A firefighter was using a hacksaw to cut the pipeline about twelve inches before the driver's chest. They then transported him to the hospital with a pipe sticking out of his chest.

During this time, dispatch had been trying to get a hold of me for an update. I had ignored the radio because of the scene, so a second deputy was dispatched to check on me. After the call, I went to the hospital and went into the emergency room. The man was lying on his back with the pipe sticking out of his chest about one foot. He was conscious, and his wife was holding his hand. I talked with the doctor who looked at the Xray and told me that the pipe went completely through his chest and was completely embedded.

The next evening shift, I drove to the hospital to see if the man died. The doctor's assistant told me that the man had survived. I asked him how one goes about removing a pipe from a chest cavity.

He told me that he first called Dr. Woo, who is a heart specialist, to begin in surgery. One has to come in from the side. As the
pipe is pulled out, the doctor has to start sewing up chest internals
so the victim does not bleed to death. Finally, they sewed up the side
incision. The pipe had just missed the heart.

The old Roy Rogers Museum was now a bowling alley at the
time. I made contact there weeks later to ask about the victim.
Apparently, the man was answering to a burglar alarm. When he
approached the business, he turned off his headlights and drove
around the back to surprise the burglar. He accidently drove through
the chain-linked fence and thus the accident. The miracle was that
he was bowling again after three weeks. An answer to prayer by the
wife and friends.

Remember; don't drive through a chain-linked fence—ever!

CHAPTER 8

---◇◈◇---

Who Ate Grandma?

I was working on day shift in the city of Hesperia. It was a clear day in the high desert. The temperature was a comfortable eighty degrees. I received a suspicious circumstance call at a house where I was to meet with the county fire department. I drove up and met with the fire captain, who asked if I had a strong stomach. I asked him why. He said that he was about to show me a human skull, which was lying on the rear backyard of the residence. I urged him to show me. He said that they came out to check on the medical well-being of an elderly woman. They found a skull and an ankle bone in the back yard. He felt it may be a burial site of a murder victim where the two dogs had dug up. I entered the backyard and met with two large, friendly dogs who seemed glad to see me. They were now tied up by the fire department. I then noted that there was a human skull lying on the lawn. I remember telling myself, "Now there's something you don't see every day." The fire captain then showed me a leg bone with the sock still on it. This was located by a shed.

I notified the dispatcher to notify homicide, who always had to leave from San Bernardino, about a forty-five-minute drive. While waiting, I noted that the rear of the house had a makeshift rear door made of plywood. The door was standing open, as if something had forced it open. The door seemed to have be nailed secure and then, later, broken apart.

I entered and noted a single bed in a side bedroom. The bed was stained, and I could smell the scent of rotted flesh. If you have ever walked by a trash can where someone had cleaned fish and threw the fish guts inside, you would know what a dead body in decay smelled like. I decided not to touch or disturb the scene anymore until homicide detectives arrived.

The homicide and crime scene unit arrived and began processing the scene. At twenty-five years old, I was eager to learn from the experienced investigators. The dogs may have been Golden Retrievers or a mix, but they were certainly nonaggressive. The detectives surmised that Grandma had had died in bed and was in the last stages of deterioration. The dogs had basically been trapped in the house with the deceased. After a time and strong smell of rotting, the dog's appetite had grown, and the deceased no longer resembled their beloved master. Well, you know the rest of the story. I took note that the dogs were carefully trained to defecate in one corner of the yard. I stared at the dung in disbelief. How could anyone have imagined that life as we know it could end like this!

I learned later that relatives had arrived and had the dogs taken away to be euthanized. I couldn't blame them.

As a first responder to death and crime scenes, you have to maintain a professional and sensitive image to victims and witnesses. Also, you have to maintain a credible, concise testimony in court.

You also have to develop a sense of humor when dealing with morbid situations. If you don't, you will either be in a shrink's office or sitting in a bar and crying in your beer. Your next call may be on violent disturbance or a sensitive rape investigation. It's best to have a sense of humor and not to take life too seriously. Years later, I would need to help a fellow detective who was having problems with panic attacks. He took the job too seriously, and I worked with him to calm him down and learn to laugh at oneself. In the end, none of us are going to survive our physical life. If you're spiritually dense, this could quite frightening. If you're a believer in Christ, this is only the beginning of something much better.

*****

My very first homicide call had been at a house in Hesperia. The suspect was a counselor of a group home, and an argument had developed over loud music. The youth had grabbed a fish fillet knife and was threatening the counselor. The counselor had gotten the knife away, and the yelling continued. The counselor then stabbed the youth in the back, not realizing that a move like this would cause death.

The counselor now sat on the couch, crying with his face in his hands. I had him stand up and placed him in handcuffs. I advised him of the Miranda rights and had him sit down to await homicide.

I would later learn that one never gives Miranda rights at the scene. It is done at an interview room later by investigating detectives or officers. What you see on TV is never done but only for TV dramatics.

I later found out that the suspect had been employed by the county. He did a very short stay in jail, and he was reemployed by the county. I saw him working as a record's clerk in the office next to the sheriff's substation!

CHAPTER 9

---◆◆◆---

I'm the Only Sane One Out Here in the Desert!

The Goodwife

I was back out on the midnight shift. The desert was cold on this night, with no wind to speak of.

I checked out a shotgun and a Mini-14 from the store room. I carried most of my supply equipment in a square-type box, which I would put on the front seat of the patrol car. I loaded the 12 gauge shotgun shells in the chamber of the shotgun and locked in into the dash-mounted holder. The Mini-14, which is basically an assault weapon, I kept in the trunk. The round placed in this weapon was a .223 caliber bullet. I logged on as Paul 7 and went 10-8, meaning in-service and available.

I immediately got a call to respond to a house address in the city of Hesperia. I was responding from Victorville substation. The call was to assist in an attempted homicide. I arrived and met with a detective in the master bedroom. He had latex gloves on and was pulling some goo off the wall.

He said that it was part of the husband's stomach which had been blown onto the wall by a shotgun blast. The detective was placing the guts into a sandwich bag for evidence.

He explained that the wife had found out that he was having an affair with another woman. While the husband decided to retire for the evening and the wife gave no indication of the affair, he felt safe to finally rest for the evening. The wife had different thoughts. She obtained the single-shot 12 gauge shotgun and carefully and calmly loaded one shell into the chamber. She placed a few more shells into her house coat pocket just in case she missed on the first few shots. She calmly approached the bedroom where her beloved husband was laying. He was on his back with his large belly inflating and then deflating on each breath. He looked like an innocent angel just beginning to fall into a deep relaxing sleep. She pointed the shotgun at his generous tummy and squeezed the trigger.

Kaboom—the shotgun went off, striking him in the stomach. Stomach innards were blown onto the wall.

The husband grabbed his stomach and saw that his petite, quiet wife was standing over him with the shotgun. He immediately ran out of the room and out of the house where he found himself on the street. He guessed that his wife must have found out about the affair. He hid himself in the shadows to observe that the petite wife, dressed only in a night gown and slippers, was outside and stalking him. She stopped to load another round into the chamber before continuing the hunt.

The husband ran to a neighbor to call the sheriff's department. Deputies arrived and placed the woman under arrest. I was assigned to transport the woman to jail.

I met with the deputy and noted a calm and polite woman dressed in her nighttime attire. She said nothing and knew she was going to jail. The deputy had to release his handcuffs so I could place my own handcuffs on her. She requested that before I place her in cuffs, she wanted to turn down the thermostat so their PG&E bill would not be high at the end of the month since no one would be home.

Wow! Talk about being conscientious and thoughtful. See, she wasn't all bad, and the husband later gained full recovery!

Guess what? After a short stay in jail, the couple got back together. And I'm guessing the PG&E bill for that month was quite low. I have no idea how the husband ever felt safe again with his wife sleeping next to him. Sure, he got rid of the shotgun, but there was still a drawer in the kitchen filled with knives. I bet when she got up in the middle of the night to use the restroom, he probably had to keep one eye open at all times.

*****

Married Couples that "Stick" Together

Another time, I got a call to a domestic violence call in Apple Valley. I rang the doorbell, and a man answered the door. One deputy stood behind me as backup. A woman stood at the back of him with a bloody nose. She was crying. He attempted to slam the door on me, but I kicked the door open and drew my .357 revolver on him. I placed him in handcuffs and transported him to the Victorville subjail. While driving, I noted that he had at one time been arrested for stabbing her with a knife.

I asked him how he could stab his own wife. He said that she had stabbed him before on another incident, so he felt it was now his turn to be the avenger. I asked if he felt it would be time for a divorce, but he said, "No, we love each other!" Wow! Talk about commitment! Through sickness and health till homicide do you part.

*****

Peacefully Deceased

I had a dead person call in Apple Valley while I was on swing shift. I was assigned to go to the hospital and sit with a homicide victim until the coroner could arrive. A nurse showed me to a room in which there was a young man lying on his back. He had reddish hair with a beard. His hair was somewhat long. The deputy I was relieving explained the story. Apparently, the deceased lived next door to a man in Apple Valley. They did not get along, and there were continuous fights and arguments between both households. On this occasion, the victim saw the other man in his own front yard. The victim went over and began screaming at the man. Apparently, this man had

had enough. The man pulled out a gun and shot the victim in the mouth while the victim was still yelling at him. This victim now lay peacefully resting on the bed to await the coroner.

I have had to sit with many dead bodies to await release to a coroner or mortuary employee. During that time, I have sat and looked at the person, wondering what their life had been like during their lifetime: their successes and their failures, etc. What had they achieved? This person, who obviously appeared peaceful now, was apparently a trouble rouser who thrived on conflict. He must have had a lot of time on his hands. He probably used drugs and lived off some type of welfare through a girlfriend or his mommy. I wondered how his final interview went with his maker. Would he make it into paradise? He was certainly not going to cause any more problems in this physical life.

The Bible mentioned loving your neighbor. John Wayne said, "Life's tough. It's tougher if you're stupid."

In fifth grade, I remember a class that taught us about drugs and their harmfulness and addictive qualities.

I did not think they were trying to keep something wonderful from us. Drugs must be bad for you. I was only ten years old when I realized that I would not be putting that crap into my body. Yet here I was sitting with a young adult man who apparently used drugs and made nothing of his life.

What a waste of an intelligent human being. I have heard all the excuses of why someone starts using drugs, but in the end, John Wayne was right. We do have free will. We are not powerless; some are just plain stupid.

Imagine, you are born with a brain capable of learning several different languages and also getting a doctor's degree in a subject that interests you. And this is what became of him! I have been stupid in life in a few of my decisions, but the difference is that I have learned from those mistakes and built from them. There is a huge increase in the number of stupid people like this moron because of the number of welfare parents having large families. It was not meant to be this way. Our government began handing out welfare in 1964 like it was candy. President Johnson started it, hoping to give people like this a "hand up." The government knew that it would aid the democratic vote, and now in 2017, the descendants have taken it to a new level and feel that welfare is a right.

Also, a new drug came in to play with stupid people. It's called meth! Not only are teenagers taking it, but young and old, hard workers and lazy individuals. Professionals and dropouts all using. Guess what? It's destroying lives, marriages, relationships, and work ethics. It is the devil's greatest achievement, and guess what? He owns you as he owns this young man, and he has come to collect! As I learned in fifth grade, do not put this into your body. It's bad. There is a spiritual world out there, and this young man just entered into it.

He better hope that death is just an eternal sleep, but I don't believe that.

At this time, I was only a very young deputy at around twenty-five years old. But I was seeing the wickedness of the world at its very ugliness. I still had about thirty more years to go before retirement. I planned on trying to stay alive and serving my community and finishing the race. My goal was to appear before God where he would say, "Well done, my faithful servant." I was hoping that he would not continue with the word *but* or *unfortunately* or something like that.

There is a phenomenon they call the crab mentality. If you have a bucket of crabs, you will never need to put a lid on it to prevent their escape. You see, when one crab begins to climb out, the others will pull the escaping crab back in. They can never escape. It works the same with people. If you grow up in a neighborhood and they decide that you should not do better than them, they'll belittle you or refuse to believe you. Jesus actually had this same problem in the neighborhood he grew up in, and he had to leave to start his ministry.

This explains why you see distant old friends after years and why rumor will cut down your accomplishments.

I went to a funeral once, and a distant friend said, "I heard you are working for the CHP." Wow! Where did that come from? "No, I work for San Bernardino sheriff's department." "Oh, what do you do?" "I sit with dead bodies, investigate murders. I place people in the hospital trying to hurt me and, sometimes, ruin their holidays. I testify in court." "Oh, you're a cop! I thought you were a dispatcher or a mechanic."

"No, sorry. I'm a person who has the power to place people in jail or prison."

My wife was accused of working for Dunkin' Donuts. Actually, she is the director of a large company.

My point is that people you grew up with can't imagine you getting ahead of them. It makes them feel uncomfortable about themselves. After all, you grew up together and had the same chance in life.

That's why you have to think bigger than where you come from. If you grew up in the ghetto, think bigger and better. Get to a library and take some time away from the "crabs" in your life. Spend extra time in class; work hard. Then guess what! You will find out that there are grants out there that will assist you in getting out of the crab pot. Don't repeat the same stupid mistakes as past generations. Don't repeat the cycle; break out of it. If all you can obtain is a job at McDonald's, then be the best and become a manager. Then go on from there. Please help our country by getting off our welfare system!

Don't end up like this man I had to sit with for two hours. Parents, quit teaching your kids hatred for wrongs that were done decades ago to older generations. I'm sorry your grandparents may have had to sit at the back of the bus. If it will make you feel better, my grandparents had to leave Ukraine. Nazi's made many people ride in cattle boxcars to death camps. I could wish that they would have been able to ride in a bus at all! Also, my last name was invented by my grandfather. It was changed to Orok so his government would not force him back. But we were never raised to hate Germans decades later. Get over it and get on with your lives; succeed in life with hard work.

Men, it's time to put your big boy pants on. It's time to be the father that you never had. If you can't do this, please don't have any kids. Our prisons and jails and welfare systems are overflowing.

For you God created my inmost being; you
knit me together in my mother's womb. I praise

you because I am fearfully and wonderfully made;
your works are wonderful, I know full well.

—Psalm 139:13–14

Now that you know what God thinks of you, let's start acting like it. Stop worrying about what the crabs think of you. When they try to pull you back into the bucket, give a good swift kick and climb on over the side. Remember, there is no lid on the bucket you may be in.

CHAPTER 10

———◇◇◇———

Assault on a Deputy

"I will meet you at the restaurant for coffee after I clear this call." I was working in the city of Hesperia on the graveyard shift. Hesperia was a city of thirty thousand residents, and I had the luxury of having another patrol unit to assist me. I was to meet with another deputy to have coffee.

It was a moonless night in the fifty-degree weather. A call came out, "Paul 6, Victorville." I answered up, "Paul 6." "Respond to 1010 7th Street for a complaint of loud music." "Paul 6 en route," I answered back to the Victorville dispatcher. "Paul 7, respond as a backup unit." "Paul 7 en route" answered Deputy Tipp.

A simple call, right? "Can you turn down the music?" I pulled in front of the house next to 1010 7th Street. I only pulled out my six-celled metal flashlight. I wouldn't need my baton, because I was here to issue a friendly verbal warning. It was 1980, and I was a twenty-five-year-old deputy.

I noted that the loud music was from a rear garage dwelling converted into a house. I opened the screen door then knocked. The door opened inwardly. A tattooed Hispanic female gang member answered the door. She saw my uniform and yelled, "The pigs!" She yanked the screen door shut and then slammed the inner door in my face. This was certainly not a taxpayer. And she was certainly not a "lady." I would see that she was treated like any other male individual. I did not want to be accused of female discrimination or male chauvinism. Deputy Tipp arrived, and I advised the senior deputy of the situation. He told me to follow him to the back door. It was unlocked!

We made entry and stood in a kitchen with tile flooring. Soon, a Mexican male, who outweighed me by about thirty pounds, ran at me with full force. There were two of us, but that only gave me a fifty percent chance of being attacked first. One thing I forgot to mention is that I am surprisingly fast!

Bruce Lee would be proud of my moves, especially when I'm terrified. Anyway, he came lunging at me, but I sidestepped to keep his body momentum continuing and bopped him over the head with my metal flashlight. He looked like Harrison Ford coming in for an almost perfect landing at LAX. I would give it an eight on a scale from one to nine. He was asleep before he hit the runway. I did not have time to see blood exiting his head wound because I was way too busy. The man had gone from rage to sleeping in out half a second.

The senior deputy stood frozen and was little use for helping me. In another second, a second Mexican ran at me and pushed me backwards over the kitchen sink. His hands were trying to claw my eyes out. The princess who had slammed the door in my face went low and grabbed for my crotch area. It was bed time for these folks as well. I smacked the lowlife over the forehead, and he went down like a sack of potatoes. He was asleep before he hit the ground. I'd give it a four for gracefulness.

The princess saw that her male homey was asleep and made a run for it. She also needed something to remember me on this night. She received a bopped to the back of her head and kept running.

Whoops; not hard enough. The senior deputy was finally recovering from shock and was able to help me with the assailants. Other deputies began to arrive from Victorville. We loaded the two unconscious males and one wounded female into the back of my patrol car and took them to Apple Valley Hospital.

I thought I had killed both as they did not regain consciousness at this time. I'm not sure why we never called for an ambulance. This was 1980 in the Wild West desert. Anyway, it was a quiet drive, and the princess did not have anything more to say to me. I took them into the emergency room, and they were given a smelling solution to help them out of their deep sleep. Hair had to be shaven off their heads, and numerous stitches to close the wounds. They would later be transferred to Victorville jail for booking.

Later, other deputies would report that these individuals were quite compliant with their dealings with police. If only they had received a decent upbringing when they were young.

This was not police brutality. This was survival, fighting for my life and well-being. Like I had said earlier in this book, I was here to survive and not get beat up. I was there for the purpose of making sure that the music was turned down. They chose to make it something bigger. They got their wish.

Imagine the first hoodlum, and let's try to get into his brain. He's brought up on the welfare system with no integrity or rules nor is he equipped to live in a civilized society. Rules mean nothing to him.

If their loud music is bothering the neighbors, too bad. Now, he's at a party, and he's enjoying himself.

He has put drugs and alcohol into his body, and he's feeling pretty good. There's a knock at the door, and he hears his female homey yell, "Pigs." They're waiting for the front door to come crashing in.

Instead, he hears two deputies in the kitchen. He runs in the kitchen and lunges full force at the smallest deputy. Oh no! Where did he go? The last thing he remembers is a bomb going off in his head. Next, he's waking up with a bright light flashing in his eyes. A voice is asking him if he remembers his name. It's the doctor, and he's in a hospital emergency room. A deputy is also present and reminding him that his next trip will be to jail.

The second gang member is also enjoying himself at the party when some pigs have come to destroy his fun. The door is slammed, securing them for at least two to three minutes. Maybe they will just go away?

No! They're in the rear kitchen, and his male homey runs at the deputy. The brute deputy does some Bruce Lee tactics, and his fellow soldier is slain across the kitchen floor. With drugs and alcohol in his system, he pushes the deputy toward the sink. He thinks to himself, *I'll gouge his eyes out!* The next thing he knows, a bomb is going off in his head. He remembers waking up to a bright light in his face. A voice is asking him if he knows his name. He notices he's talking to the emergency doctor. His head is aching.

A deputy is also standing by, and his wrist is handcuffed to the bed rail.

The princess answers the front door. There is a deputy standing outside. She grabs the screen door to slam it. She yells "pigs" for the courtesy of anyone having drugs to start hiding them. She slammed the inner door and locked it. This will give them at least one to two minutes before the front door comes crashing in. Hopefully, someone brought a gun to defend themselves. The next thing the princess hears is her homey running to the rear door. It's like a scene of *Enter the Dragon* starring Bruce Lee. Her homey is knocked out stone cold. The other father of her children is enraged just like she is. There must be some way she can help the cause. Yes, while her children's father is blinding the deputy, she can come in low and grab his male organs. Oh no! Father number two falls onto the floor. Quick, run! She feels the back of her head explode. Luckily, she's too stupid to go unconscious.

She is escorted to the back of a patrol car. She hopes that the fathers of her children are not deceased.

Someday, all three members will have great stories to tell their grandchildren. Great party!

Deputy Tipp lasted about three more years before he resigned and began working for Coca-Cola. Good, the job was not for him. Another deputy named Von Elmer said that he would never have hit the suspects in the manner I did. He was quite confident in himself and bragged about his football career in high school.

One year later, he was inside an apartment. He and Deputy Bamley were there to arrest a parolee on a warrant. The problem was that the parolee did not wish to go back to prison. This was not a football game either. There are no rules and fouls.

Deputy Von Elmer went to place the parolee in handcuffs. The parolee got up and knocked Deputy Von Elmer backward. The deputy fell back and hit his head on a coffee table. He was knocked out cold and useless. The parolee was now in a position to grab his gun to use on Deputy Bamley.

Deputy Bamley pulled his gun and convinced the parolee to go into custody.

A few days later, the newspaper came out, and on the front page was Deputy Von Elmer being wheeled out on a gurney, and he was holding his own IV bag. He had a dumb look on his face, and I could almost see two blue birdies flying around his head in a circle, just like in the cartoons I used to watch. His mouth was opened in a confused manner, and his eyes were wide and confused. He looked like an NFL linebacker had just laid him out.

When he had gotten better, I explained, "Now you know why I go into survival mode!" Luckily, Deputy Bamley had saved the overconfident deputy's life! I kept a copy of the newspaper article to remind myself how our job is so dangerous, and we only have a second to react.

*****

Finally, court came for the three hoodlums. I dressed in a suit with a tie. We had the option of wearing a suit or a uniform. Deputy Tipp wore his uniform. As we walked into the court hallway, one of the gang members spoke out, "Look, he needs an armed security to protect him!" Apparently, his memory wasn't too keen. No wonder why these creatures always get into fights and drive-by shootings against other opposing gang members. They can't seem to keep their mouths shut.

In court, I testified about the night in question. The judge didn't like the fact that we went through the unlocked back door. You see, in court you will find out that you violated some ridiculous rule where one only has seconds to respond while out in the streets. Apparently, he found that we violated the knock-and-notice ruling when making the arrests. The prosecuting attorney was also stunned and asked the judge what the officers should have done.

The judge stated that when the door was slammed in the deputies' faces, the deputies should have yelled out, "We're here to make arrests," then kicked the front door in. This would have been a legal entry. Then arrests would have been lawful.

Hey! I thought, *Why kick a perfectly good door in when one can merely walk to the unlocked back door and get inside?* Apparently, the judge was not a landlord. Not to mention officer safety reasons.

Anyway, the criminal case was dismissed. Then the sharks appeared, all hungry and going after the civil case that would ensue. Hungry sharks better known as attorneys. Wow, this would net them some income, maybe payoff the car loan or merely the PG&E bill. Maybe get creditors off their backs.

Finally, some income coming in. Each shark knew they would get about a third of whatever the settlement brought in. This was truly a good day for any "legal prostitute" who could call these hoodlums, "clients."

Some would probably fantasize about that dream vacation in the Caribbean, all paid for by tax-paying Citizens. Actually, a county will pay lawsuits with an insurance policy. Anyway, maybe a Hawaiian trip.

The county hired an attorney for me. His office was located in Los Angeles. I had to drive into LA to my attorney's office. I believe his name was Bailey. The hoodlum's attorney was also present and starved-looking. I thought about maybe giving her a few dollars for lunch. This was in regards to what they call a deposition hearing.

The hoodlum's attorney started asking me questions about that fateful night. I explained in full detail about the "Battle of the Alamo." I explained how goodness had prevailed, not to mention that the music had gotten turned down and peace and quiet were restored to the taxpayers.

My attorney remained quiet and allowed me to answer questions. At one point, he interrupted and stated, "Counselor, your clients sound like a bunch of lowlifes!" The attorney ignored the comment and kept thinking more about the money that would soon be coming in. At one point, the attorney asked, "Deputy, where was your baton during this incident?"

Can you believe it? She wanted me to hit them with my baton after the "Bruce Lee" I performed on their crowns with a flashlight! Hadn't they suffered enough because of their transgressions? If she dares ask me why I hit them with my flashlight, I was ready to announce, "In the position your clients had me in, I couldn't get to my gun. I had to settle for my flashlight, but it proved quite sufficient."

Anyway, my attorney advised me not to answer the question. They argued for several minutes, and soon, my deposition was over. I walked into five o'clock Friday night traffic in downtown Los Angeles in order to battle the delightful traffic congestion. I was completely overtaken by the beauty of the smog-filled air of the "City of the Angels," as well as the parking lot that was meant to be a freeway.

Later, I learned that the county had made out a payout of $10,000 to dismiss the case, even though the sheriff's office decided I had been in the right. I heard mention that the hoodlums had told a deputy to thank Orok for the boat he bought with my settlement!

Let's do the math. $10,000 and the attorney gets about $3,333. The attorney will have numerous tax write-offs and will keep most of that money. The hoodlums are left with $6,667 and have to divide that three ways. So each hoodlum now makes $2,222 each. Okay, but here comes the government, and he wants to be paid. Hoodlums usually don't have any tax write-off, because they don't work, so probably forty percent has to be paid to Uncle Sam. So $900 to Uncle Sam per hoodlum times three or $2,700 total to the government.

That leaves only $1,322 per hoodlum. That's only enough to buy a plastic kayak at Walmart or an inflatable raft from a Camel cigarettes catalog. You might be able to buy an old aluminum boat that will have to be powered by oars. With the rest of the money, they could buy a case of beer, carton of cigars, and drugs, but that's it!

The best thing they get to keep is the healed over scars on their heads that they can proudly show their grandchildren someday. The true winners are the attorney at $3,333, and the government with a close second at $2,700. "Case dismissed!"

I want to be clear on the use of force. I wasn't a bully or using unusual force. I was Davy Crockett, and I was battling for my very own life. There's a difference. In the end, everyone was a winner.

The attorney was able to pay for her late car payments, the government got a healthy portion, the hoodlums got an inflatable boat, and I got to keep my life. Oh, and don't forget, the music was finally turned down.

CHAPTER 11

—◇◆◇—

George Air Force Base

B efore I begin, let me say how grateful I am for our armed service men and women. You keep our country safe from the wolves who wish to do us harm. You are either in harm's way constantly or you're helping the effort. Your job is important. It's a hard job, and you do it for low pay and frugal retirement benefits. Your families also suffer from long deployments, constant relocating, and a dismal W-2 at the end of the year. Many spouses have to become both mother and father while their spouse is away. Once again, you have my deepest appreciation. Thank you.

George Air Force Base was located in Victorville on the outskirts in the 1980s. It is presently a private air base now. During that time, I got to work with air personnel who were reserves with the sheriff's department, and unfortunately, I got to arrest a few members of the Air Force.

I was surprised by how stupid some were and also on the arrogance of the pilots and officers. They're big shots on base, but off base, some needed to be reminded that they were just ordinary people with no horsepower. All of them went into handcuffs just like anyone else. When the air base called the jail every morning at four a.m., they wanted to know if any airmen were in custody. The airmen were twice as afraid from the punishment they would receive from base than from civil courts.

I remember having a pilot who was the rear seat and navigator in a phantom jet. He became a reserve deputy and was quite arrogant. He was allowed to man a patrol car and quickly wrecked the vehicle in a collision. He thought he would get another vehicle and a salute to go with it. Instead, he got a boot out the door and was not allowed to continue as a reserve deputy.

Another occasion found me pulling over a drunk driver who I learned was a German fighter pilot.

I loved his German accent. I like to jokingly talk with my customers. But no harm; I treat everyone fairly. I joked, "Hey, you're German. Last time I looked, weren't you the guys who started a World War or two?" He explained that the American government trained German fighter pilots so they could patrol the Russian border and help protect us.

While I was processing his booking paperwork, I asked him if he would say "sign zee papers" with the heavy German accent. I explained that I've seen movies where the German government would always say that.

He refused, and I told him that I wrote slower when I was upset and it would take longer to process him.

He immediately gladly said, "Sign zee papers."

I said, "That was great. Thank you. I'll get you processed in no time." Actually, I was trying to calm his frightful situation while in custody with mild teasing. I was hoping that he would take it well if someday he might be flying over my patrol car in a phantom and decide it was payback time.

*****

While working day shift on a beautiful and clear morning, I was working in the city limits of Victorville. About nine a.m., I received a call of an attempted theft of tires from the Holiday Inn Restaurant on 7th Street. The waitress explained that while serving customers, another employee asked her if someone was repairing her car. After saying no, she walked out to the parking lot and saw an airman dressed in class B fatigues uniform trying to remove her wheels with a lug wrench.

She yelled, "Hey, what are you doing to my car?" The airman said oh and jumped into a minitruck.

The waitress wrote down the license plate and noted that there was an Air Force sticker on the bumper and windshield.

It's time like this that I feel my job was just too easy. Couldn't he wait for darkness like a normal crook? Maybe dress in a dark turtleneck sweater and wool cap? Anyway, I had my dispatcher call the air base's front security gate. They were given the vehicle description and said that the driver was under arrest for attempted theft. The crook left a few minutes prior so he should be arriving momentarily. As expected, the base called and said that I had another customer in custody. I arrived fifteen minutes later and saw an airman handcuffed. He was standing with two base security police, and they both held M16 rifles. While en route to the jail, I announced that he had unofficially qualified as the dumbest crook in the high desert.

OSI personnel investigate criminal matters in the armed forces. I met with the officer who is also a reserve deputy. After bailing the airman from the jail, the Air Force transported him to the military jail, where he could be properly interrogated without silly constitutional rights. He actually confessed to a few robberies on base.

*****

There was an incident where several women had been raped around the Victorville city limits over the span of several weeks. A drawing of the suspect and been made, and it was printed in the high desert newspaper.

One female victim had been standing in line in a local bank when she identified the suspect, also a customer standing in line. The victim immediately called the sheriff's office, and the suspect was arrested.

It was found out that the suspect was an airman who lived in the base. He was married and had two young children. Who would have guessed? This job kept getting more and more interesting.

*****

I was working swing shift and on patrol. Sometime during the spring and as luck would have it, I was the only patrol car out for both Hesperia and Apple Valley. Both cities were each about thirty thousand in population. When working for the county, one gets shorthanded, and they have to make do. I was getting multiple violent calls, and the dispatcher was trying to manage the calls through priority standards. Also, when the desert gets hot in temperature, everyone's temper gets short, including mine. When you say something inappropriate, then the office is called, and then one has to answer to the sergeant or, worse, internal affairs in San Bernardino.

On days like this, I've often wondered if $14.00 an hour was really worth it. The driver for Wonder Bread made $15.00 an hour. Why was I doing this? The county provided us with an underpowered Ford Fairmont with poor air conditioning system.

I had gotten one call with an obnoxious individual and my rear end was still burning from the insults when I received another disturbance call with two neighbors arguing. I was at my wit's end. I approached the scene and got out of the patrol car. They began yelling at me, and I still hadn't recovered from the last call. Out of frustration, I said, "Look, I just came from an offending call, and my rear end was still burning. I don't want to do something stupid or make a bad arrest! I'm going to try to come up with a solution, but I am all out of patience. Please work with me!"

You know what? This actually works, and it is the only way one can survive this type of work. Learn to talk; tell the other party what mental state you're in. I actually learned this in jail when talking with an inmate. He said that when you come to work and are in a bad mood, let us know, and we will stay out of your way. Apparently, some deputies were coming to work with personal issues and taking it out on the inmates.

While talking to the two neighbors in Hesperia, I got a call to respond to Apple Valley because of a disturbance with possible shots fired. I had no backup and would be responding alone, as usual. I arrived to a duplex unit and knocked on the door of the disturbance. It was quiet and no one answered the door. I heard music from the adjoining from apartment and knocked on this door. An airman answered the door with three other airmen. I immediately smelled marijuana and decided to ignore the offense. I asked if they had heard gunshots next door, which they explained that they hadn't. I believed them to be credible witnesses, because they were servicemen serving our country. If a gunshot had gone off, these fine men would have heard something.

It was at this time in my career when I learned that maybe I was giving the armed service a little too much credit for some of the members having any means of intelligence. For the men in the Army, don't say anything about the Air Force. Private Bergdahl deserted the base, and they promoted him to sergeant while AWOL! Our then president traded him for several dangerous terrorists.

Anyway, it was quiet at the scene, and if anything else happened, I felt that members of the Armed Forces would call back. I proceeded back to the original disturbance to stop those neighbors from killing each other. Guess what! The dispatcher announced that the neighbors had worked things out and had no more need of my services. My counseling had worked. I had no more disturbance calls pending. Being a deputy was one of the hardest police work I have done in my thirty-two-year career. It was brutal, and the pay was low.

A few days later, I learned that someone went back to the Apple Valley call and found that on that disturbance call, the roommate had shot his friend and then himself. Homicide came up from San Bernardino and questioned the airmen. OSI also came up. I heard that the airmen had gotten into trouble and possibly expelled from the Air Force.

I felt that I would be called into the captain's office for not investigating properly, but the call never came. They knew I was doing the best I could for a deputy overworked and covering two cities at the same time.

My conscience was bothering me, and the captain assured me that there would have been nothing I could have done for the deceased. From then on in, I would never leave a scene on a call like this one without breaking a window or forcing a door to check. Even with airmen next door hearing no gun shots, I would still force entry to be sure. Then if the entry was unwarranted, I would then have to write a memo for damaged property.

CHAPTER 12

———◇◇◇———

Tracking Shoe Prints

One of my favorite services of detective work was tracking. I had joined the police world to investigate. I had no idea I would be in patrol, in uniform for as long as I did. But as a somewhat rural deputy, I could investigate all my reported crimes. There was just too much work to go around, and the detectives here were snowed under with paperwork. They appreciated my help and merely had to walk my reports over to the district attorney's office for review and further action from there.

I hated to see victims' residences broken into. Personal and irreplaceable items and treasures were stolen. But the most important of all, their kingdom was invaded and violated. Their place of refuge and safety was violated. One would never feel safe again once the door was locked, fearing that the violator would revisit them at any hour. Every strange noise or sound would be suspect.

Although the courts only look at burglary as a mere property crime, the fear and empty feeling leaves a victim feeling similar to that of a rape victim but not as intense. This is why I don't know why more burglars are not shot on sight. They may be unarmed, but once inside, they merely have to visit the kitchen to obtain knives, and they're free to rape or murder if they wish to.

When someone enters your house without your permission, they are dangerous. Let's start treating them accordingly and not mere property offenders. Remember, you have to be in fear of your life or that of your family.

I went to law school for one semester and remember having to brief a case involving a store owner who placed a bear trap in his business after closing. The only one who would get trapped would be a burglar. Guess what? It worked! Couldn't get better, right? I'm sorry to say that the owner was sued and lost. I can only hope that the attorney, judge, or anyone responsible for the findings will have their businesses broken into. Anyway, as you can tell, I'm a victim's advocate. I've never had my home broken into, but I've experienced many people who have. I feel helpless when I cannot help the victim and add to the population of the prison system.

I learned tracking in the academy during only one class. I became amused and knew this was my calling in the art of investigation. Most crooks are unaware of their foot tracks, concentrating on mostly on their fingerprints. In a rural area, when a crime is committed in a burglary, one can tell the point of entry, the number of suspects, the placement of a getaway car sometimes leading the investigator right to the crook's home. It can also be used to disqualify a false report of robbery or attempted rape. With the photo of the foot track and the suspect's shoes, you can place him at the scene. Defense attorneys hated when their clients were facing charges with my name at the bottom of the report as being the investigator. One attorney actually told me that he admired my skills and testimony expertise. He then told me he would have to try to rip me up on the stand and not to take it personally. He admitted that he would probably lose the case, but his job was to protect his client. Guess what? He lost.

*****

On a dayshift call, I received a burglary complaint at an address in Apple Valley. I had a teenaged male explorer riding with me. He looked to be athletic and possibly into high school sports. The victim explained that her parrot and cage had been taken. I asked if she noticed any open doors or windows upon arriving home. A window in the rear had been forced open, and the front door was found unlocked. I checked with neighbors, but none had seen anything. I found the shoe tracks leading to the rear bedroom window. I obtained my foot track camera stand and camera and took a photo of the track, one with a ruler, another without the ruler to show the actual size. I then sketched, measured, and noted characteristics of the shoe tracks, drawing each characteristic in the picture.

When tracking, this will help one when looking for the particular track and seeing others in a busy intersection when some tracks may look similar. I began tracking the suspect walking down the street.

When coming to an intersection, it was sometimes difficult when the suspect crossed the paved roadway. It took patience, and the explorer stayed on the opposite side of the street until the foot track was picked up again. We followed the track for several intersections, and for what seemed to be a mile or two, we were able to have it lead us to a house. Bingo!

I radioed dispatch of my location and requested a supervisor meet with us and also an additional deputy if one was available. This was going to be so fun! It's the look on the crook's face when you inform him that you tracked him. Imagine, before opening the door, he could hide the parrot, but he would not be able to hide that big wire cage. The sergeant responding was familiar with my tracking ability, so I know he was pumped too.

The sergeant arrived, and I knocked on the front door, and this is the best part! The crook answered, and I advised that I wanted the parrot back. "What parrot? What makes you think I have a parrot?"

I announced, "I'm a tracker for the San Bernardino sheriff's department, and I tracked you here."

I like sounding official, and so I included the long title, and I thought this would increase my credibility with the soon-to-be inmate. The crook looked at me as if I was nuts or joking. I mean, come on, tracking only happens on television with an Indian guide doing the tracking, right?

Anyway, he said that we would need a warrant. The sergeant announced that the crook would have to wait on the porch until the warrant arrived. I advised, "Look, I only want to get the bird back to the owner. It's no big thing." I always tried to downplay the crime so the crook could confess easier. He then announced that we could go inside. I found the bird cage in a rear room without the bird inside. I asked the crook, "You flushed the bird down the toilet?" He then said, "I let him go in the attic."

Guess who got to go into the attic? Remember, it's hot, stuffy, and one must remember to keep on the beams to avoid crashing through the plaster board and landing to the floor underneath.

No, I didn't ask the explorer, and I couldn't ask for this. Even better! He volunteered. Armed with a heavy glove and expert advice, he made me proud that day, and we returned the parrot to the cage.

The sergeant was happy. I was happy. The explorer was happy and learned not to be the first to volunteer anymore. The owner was happy. The crook probably felt stupid.

Case cleared by arrest. Suspect in custody.

*****

I had responded to an assault with a deadly weapon call in a rural section of Apple Valley located on a hillside. The man had blood on his forehead. He explained that he had gotten into an argument with his daughter and her boyfriend. The boyfriend had hit him with a stick across the victim's head.

He explained that they had walked off into the desert and pointed out the direction.

I found the suspect's and daughter's shoe tracks and began following them along the hillside. The tracks led up to a cabin. I was not going to search the cabin alone and was not sure if I needed to call for another deputy as once again, we were shorthanded. I wanted to eliminate the cabin as a hiding place in case they were not inside, but I didn't want to expose myself to harm by being alone.

I made a wide circle around the cabin and checked for tracks. I picked up the tracks once again heading away from the cabin, so I now knew they had passed the cabin and not gone inside. I continued to follow the tracks along the hillside where they finally ended at a large bush.

Then I withdrew my .357 Smith & Wesson and pointed it at the bush. I announced, "Sheriff's department. Come out with your hands up." The bushes moved, and both young adults came out. I placed handcuffs on the male in front of him. We had a long walk back, and if he stumbled, I did not want him falling on his face. The female walked behind the suspect. I transported the male suspect to Victorville substation jail for assault with a deadly weapon. The suspect seemed stunned that he could be tracked across the desert and found hiding under a bush.

*****

My tracking abilities also enabled me to tell when a person was lying. I was working on a graveyard shift in Apple Valley. There was a second deputy also working. Deputy Ren got a call of a robbery at a small liquor store in a small plaza area. The wind had been blowing that night, smoothing out old foot tracks and making a clean sheet of the dirt and sand.

The store clerk had told Deputy Ren that a suspect came into the store and demanded money from the cash register. The suspect showed the clerk a gun. The clerk then gave $120.00 to the suspect, who then fled out the door and ran to the back of the complex. I arrived and had the clerk show me exactly which direction the suspect had gone. While Deputy Ren was taking the report, I was checking for shoe tracks. Guess what? There were no tracks present. I told Ren that the clerk was lying and left the deputy to complete his report.

Later, I heard Ren on his radio announcing that he was 10-15, meaning one in custody, en route to Victorville subjail. Deputy Ren later told me that he interrogated the clerk, who finally admitted to sticking the $120.00 in his shoe and calling in a false report of a robbery.

Money recovered, cleared by arrest.

*****

Residential Burglary (Twice):
Time to Send in the Big Guns

I was back on swing shift, working in the city of Hesperia on a windless, clear evening. It was a pleasant evening; the type of evening that made one want to possibly go on a walk. Hesperia has a mesa area that I learned to love so well. The high beautiful mountains of the San Bernardino Mountains stood in the background. I had actually bought my first house here on a hilly residential street with a big, one-acre parcel of land.

I received a call, "Paul 6, Victorville." I responded, "Go ahead, Victorville." "Paul 6, respond to 20230 Spruce street in regards to a residential PC 459," meaning burglary. "Paul 6, copy." I drove to the location and made contact with a young couple who explained that this was the second time that their house had been burglarized in one week.

Why weren't the crooks caught on the first report? The crooks left the same evidence as the one I was now investigating. The deputy who had taken the first report had taken the same tracking class that I had in the academy. The reason, I believe, is that the deputy did the minimum work and went 10-8, "Back in Service," writing the report, possibly sketching a foot track—but the bare minimum amount of investigating. I don't know why officers do the bare minimum. Don't they like investigating and putting people in handcuffs in the back seat of their patrol cars? Recovering property for the victims? I live in a city of about seventy-six thousand people between Stockton and Modesto, and the police here do the least they can do. I've shown them crooks stealing my neighbors' car via my security camera. I told them that the crook lived nearby in an abandoned motorhome and looked like Matt Damon's little brother but was told that they would only forward the report to an auto task force.

Didn't the officer want to make an arrest? Was it the liberal judges who have been placing car thieves on probation with no jail time served?

Are not officers and deputies rated for their arrests and investigation skills anymore? Maybe the officers with great skills are transferred to specialized units where the general public doesn't meet on regular calls for service, leaving the lazy officer or deputy to deal with the public.

Anyway, back to burglary in Hesperia. I noted that the crooks went through a rear window. I sketched and photographed and measured three different pairs of foot tracks. I left my patrol car parked in the driveway with the window down next to the porch area. The radio also remained on. Without taking down enough information, I began tracking the suspects. I needed them to be in jail before sunrise so they wouldn't miss breakfast. Actually, I love arresting crooks!

I tracked these defendants, two to three blocks to a house. The garage door was open, and three teenaged males were shooting a BB gun in the garage. I had to walk down the block to see what street I was on. I noted the address number on the crook's house. I radioed dispatch for additional units and a sergeant. I asked dispatch to call the victim back and ask if BB guns were stolen. The dispatcher said that the victim called and said they had stolen BB guns, all before the call was made.

I wondered if the victim was reading my mind somehow. I later found that the victim couple had been sitting on the porch, listening to my radio, and immediately called when they heard my request.

Units came from Apple Valley and Victorville. In the still night, one could hear the four barrels on the carburetors kicking in as the deputies accelerated the patrol cars and began arriving. For the newer generation, the carburetor is what was used before fuel injection was invented. For the even newer generation, it's a thing under the hood of a car.

Contact was made with the defendants. Jewelry, BB guns, and all items that they just had to have were recovered and placed in evidence. The three defendants were booked into jail and juvenile hall and, as far as I know, didn't miss breakfast.

The victims were more than excited! They said they never seen anything like it, listening to the professionals going into action. It beat anything that was on TV that night. This was the real thing.

Their adrenalin was pumping. They had front row seats without the immediate danger present.

Most important, their property was recovered! They were going to write a letter to the sheriff expressing their gratitude! Almost forty years later, I'm still waiting for that letter.

*****

Tracking suspects can also get you killed. Always remember to look up.

When tracking potentially armed suspects, a deputy should have a spotter who is looking out for threats while the tracker can concentrate on the track and direction it is traveling.

Jake Phillips was constantly causing grieve and disturbances with his circle of friends and acquaintances.

He would cause trouble and strife wherever he went. He would try to control former girlfriends and friends.

He was known to carry a 9mm pistol. When police were called, he could hear the patrol cars coming and hide in whatever space he could crawl into. Once, he hid in an outside water heater closet.

On this night, Jake tried to cause an apparent disturbance at an ex-girlfriend's house, located in Hesperia. I drove up and noted no evidence of him still being in the area as I spoke with the resident. Sgt. Wellington arrived, as did two other deputies. Sgt. Wellington was presently a tactical leader for the new ERT, meaning emergency response team. This was a team who would be deployed until the SWAT team could arrive from San Bernardino, forty miles away.

With the suspect still at large, the sergeant noticed an abandon house across the street. He felt that the suspect might be hiding in the house, and he also saw a training opportunity for the team members. I decided to track the suspect instead. The other deputies had already crossed the street and were making entry to the house. I located the suspect's track and began to follow it.

Kaboom—came from the house across the street as I heard the shotgun go off. I thought, *Oh, they must have located the suspect, and he's now in heaven, or not.* I continued to track and noted that the shoe tracks ended at car tracks. This would indicate that the suspect was picked up by a car. I gave no notice to the tree where the car tracks were located.

The good sergeant came back, and I asked if they had found the suspect. He explained that the house was clear and that it was an accidental discharge. Well, I said, "I guess the team needs more practice?"

I cleared the call and left the scene.

The next evening, I learned that I would be working in the subjail. Jake Phillips was now in custody, and he would be my guest of honor. Another shift had caught him in another complaint call. I was excited to talk with him. I explained that I was the deputy who responded to the previous evening.

Jake stated, "You know, that was the funniest call I ever seen deputies respond on. I could hear the units coming from a block away, so I immediately jumped onto the tree and started climbing. I felt they would look up and see me. Four deputies crossed the street, and then I heard the shotgun go off. Then they exited with dumb looks on their faces. One deputy stayed behind and tracked me right to the tree I was in. Guess what? He never even looked up! He could have had me!"

I then told Jake that I was the deputy who had tracked him. I asked him if he had the pistol on him.

He stated that he was carrying the pistol. I asked him if he would have shot me. He responded, "I don't really know."

Maybe it was good that I didn't look up. Maybe the shotgun blast had taken my concentration off the investigation. Maybe my guardian angel watched over me and made sure I didn't look up.

Anyway, from then on, I never forgot to look up.

I was a deputy working in the Wild West for San Bernardino sheriff's department. Many people say that Wyatt Earp worked for the county as a deputy. Actually, Virgil Earp, an older brother had lived in the city of Colton and was a marshal for a very brief period. He later got a job as an armed security agent working for the railway, probably because they paid better. The railway was in a dispute with a rival rail company, and Virgil tried to stop the opposing rail company. About ten San Bernardino deputies confronted Virgil with guns. Although Virgil had his gun out, he quickly backed down because he was outgunned by the deputies.

Virgil is buried in Los Angeles, and Wyatt is buried near San Francisco.

*****

Dishwasher Burglars

I was back on day shift and assigned to Apple Valley. The day was a beautiful spring day, warm temperature with no wind. "Paul 4, Victorville." I responded back, "Paul 4." "PC 459 report at 119230 Kiamichi Rd." "Paul 4, copy." I was responding to another burglary of a newly constructed and vacant house. The house was a beautiful ranch-style house that was in the process of being put on the market for sale. The owner had announced that he arrived and found that the door knob on the front door was broken and a dishwasher was taken. I noted two sets of foot tracks leading to the house.

Burglars used a set of vice locks to forcefully turn the door knob and break its locking function.

I sketched, measured, and photographed the shoe tracks and saw that the suspects had approached the rear kitchen window to view the appliances. One look at the dishwasher, and they knew that they couldn't live without it. They decided to make entry. I began tracking the shoe tracks backward and followed them to a nearby house. I then reversed and followed them towards the victim's house.

The tracks indicated that two men had walked from the house in a side by side pattern. Sometimes the tracks indicated that one suspect had walked behind the other, but there was no uniformity as they approached the victim's house. Once inside, the dishwasher was removed with both men carrying it. The tracks were now uniform and exactly three feet apart from each other, indicating that the men were carrying an object together. Imagine if one were to carry one end of a table with a helper carrying the other end across the desert. One's tracks would have to be uniform in distance from the other, somewhat like marching band. This was important, because I would later have to testify in court about this.

I made contact at the suspects' house, but no one was at home. I came back later with another deputy and arrested both suspects for burglary. I did not find the dishwasher so I assumed that it had been sold and probably installed at another home.

In the jail interview room, I interview the suspects individually. They were given their Miranda rights. Both chose to talk with me. They already had their stories made up and in place.

They explained that they had walked to the victim's house, but it was only to view the house and admire the new home. They said they only looked through the window and never made entry or stole anything. I then advised them of their shoe tracks and their position. They said it must have been just a coincidence. Later, their lawyer must have thought that it was a great story.

In court, the DA had a large paper where I could draw and the jury could see. I drew the tracks leading to the victim's house. I advised the jury that if they had walked back in the same manner, then the tracks would appear the same, with one walking a few feet in distance, sometimes four or five feet from each other. I then drew the tracks leading away, side by side from three feet apart, and in a uniform direction, indicating the carrying of the dishwasher.

During the arrest, I had taken both their shoes and showed that they matched the photographed crime scene tracks. The jury went into deliberation and found the suspects guilty of burglary. I'm sure the attorney was depressed, but he still got a retainer for trying. I wish I could have arrested him also. I could only hope that the next victim will be him.

When investigating a crime, an officer has to be prepared to testify and convince a jury of his investigation. That means writing a good report. Attorneys grew to hate when my name was on a burglary report because their work would be cut out for them. But I'm sure they appreciated the clients and income that my arrests brought them.

*****

The Deputy is Scrooge: Who Could Arrest on Christmas Day?

While working on a graveyard shift on Christmas Eve, I got a grand theft call from the garage area of a home in Apple Valley. I responded and met with a former deputy, who was now in construction work. He had gotten tired of the low pay. He said that two men had come to pick up his daughter up from the house. They left to go out on this Christmas Eve. Wendel had gone out to his garage and noticed that his tool chest and various other equipment were stolen. He had already located the tracks which led back to the front yard where they ended at the tire tracks that the guests had made. Apparently, while waiting for his daughter, the suspects decided to explore the rear and saw the garage. There were items inside that they just had to have. They loaded the items in the car before the daughter came out. Wendel gave me the name of one suspect. He didn't know the other's name.

I ran the name through records and obtained an address. The sun was coming up, and it was now Christmas Day. Excited children would be waking up to see what Santa had brought. Christians would be arising to celebrate the birth of their Savior. Christmas is, after all, a Christian celebration of the birth of Jesus. Because I usually had to work, this was my gift to the Savior. I arrested the evil, the thieves, the murderers. During Christmas holidays, crime always goes up. Suicides and murders skyrocket, as dysfunctional families get together to try and enjoy each other. Drunk driving soars as people want to be merry. This is not a day of rest for law enforcement.

I arrived at the house with two other deputies. They answered the door, hoping that Santa had forgotten to deliver more goodies. Instead, Scrooge had arrived with two other deputies. I arrested a young man and his uncle for grand theft. The owner of the house was the brother of one arrestee and the father of the younger man. He was shocked, devastated that the evil lawmen would make an arrest on Christmas morning. I would be receiving no presents on the following Christmas. Saint Nick would remember me, and I would pay big time!

We drove the defendants to the Victorville subjail. The uncle would not talk to me. I convinced the nephew to talk and show me where the loot had been stashed. We drove out to an abandoned shack with another patrol unit, and I recovered all stolen property. I drove the defendant/client back to the jail and booked him in custody. I walked by the uncle's cell and, with a very mischievous and naughty smile, announced that his nephew had told me everything.

Believe it or not, the brother came to the sheriff's station to do a complaint on me! He walked into the sergeant's office for the complaint. While walking in, he gave me the dirtiest look of distain.

I found out later that his complaint was of me making an arrest on Christmas morning and that they weren't able to open presents. The sergeant said that he was a real nice guy and sensitive but was only upset because of the timing. Couldn't I have waited until the following day?

Did his brother and son wait until after Christmas Eve to steal? What about the victim? I felt so bad about this incident, so I wanted to do something about it. I went back into the jail and walked up defendant's cell and stated, "Hey, guys, in case I forgot, Merry Christmas!" My conscious was now cleansed, and there was still a small chance that St. Nick would forget about this entire incident in the next 364 days.

CHAPTER 13

———— ◈◈◈ ————

There Are Some Seriously
Crazy People Out Here

I was working on swing shift in the city of Hesperia. It was a nice day and was not too warm. The winds were light, and evening was just an hour away. I received a call to respond to a liquor store in response to a man who was wrapped in explosives! Now, how was I going to handle this call? I guess I would just have to handle it in the best way I could invent at the moment.

On a call like this, I position myself in front of the business and try to observe the area and see what the situation is. I drove up and distanced myself from the scene and got out and stood next to my patrol car. A man in his midtwenties started to approach my car. He had long hair and looked like the typical desert low life. He spread his jacket open, and I could see that his body was wrapped with explosives. I yelled at him to stop, but he continued to my location and stood right in front of me.

Before I go on, I have to admit that this was the most terrifying moment in my entire thirty-two-year career.

I want you to know that when one is in a situation like this, all your bravado is gone. Also, you learn how to talk very fast. And one is very honest in their feelings. Anyone who says that they stared the guy down or talked tough is lying. Many would have defecated in their shorts.

I've had guns pulled on me, but nothing is as terrifying as being blown up. My heart goes out to the people who work in the bomb squad.

The first thing that came out of my mouth was, "I don't want to die!" The low life looked at me and said, "I don't want to die either." Great, I was developing human bonding with this individual.

We both didn't want to die. Things were looking up! I then inquired, "Then why are you wrapped in explosives?" He said, "I'm just messing around." I spoke, "But are those live?" He said that they weren't. *Great,* I thought, *now I could kick his ass in.*

I had him unwrap himself, and then I placed him in handcuffs in the back of my patrol car. He stated that he was a "powder monkey" and worked with road crews when something needed to be exploded during construction and road clearing. He felt it would be funny to see the expression of the liquor store clerk if he opened his jacket to let the clerk have a look. He told the clerk, "It would be a shame if this place blew up!" It was all done in fun, and if one were also nuts, you could see the humor in it.

He showed me where his car was parked, and guess what? He had a stick of dynamite balancing between the directional turn lever and the steering wheel. And I wasn't going to touch it. I notified dispatch to have the bomb squad come up from San Bernardino. I also needed an additional unit to assist me.

While I was waiting, a friend of the low life tried to open my rear door to get his friend out. I was now fighting with this moron. I requested for backup units from Victorville. A second unit showed up, and we placed moron number two in the next unit. A person of the press had heard the call on scanner and wanted to report on the action. Another low life came out of the woodwork and began swearing at the reporter. I approached the third low life, and he ran from me. I had been training with a PR-24, which is a baton with a side handle. It was made out of aluminum. I ran about a block and threw it at him. The reporter was right behind, not to let a good story escape. The baton hit the ground, sending off sparks at the violator's feet. It looked neat! The hoodlum wasn't giving up, so out of desperation, I said, "I'm sorry, but I'm going to have to shoot you." No, I would not have shot him, but I was curious if he would stop. Guess what! He stopped, fearing I would shoot him. I think by apologizing for shooting him, he felt I was quite serious. I took him into custody. Business was good tonight! The reporter got some great shots and a great story too.

The bomb squad arrived and placed a fifty-foot string around the dynamite and pulled. That's how things were done in the 1980s. We didn't have a robot. The dynamite did not explode. This was just another desert joke. The T-handle was loosened from my throwing it, so I sent it back to the factory and didn't see it for about two months. I learned never to throw it again. I would have to go back to my straight-handled wooded baton for the duration. And I was just getting good with my PR-24. Oh, well.

*****

Even the Pizza Guy's Nuts

We had a pizza business on Main St. in Hesperia. It was owned by a hyper, overzealous mid-aged nut. He felt he needed a gun in order to protect his business. He applied for a concealed weapons permit, and guess what? They gave it to him. Actually, the county of San Bernardino sheriff granted it. I guess it didn't require a pysch test. Anyway, the pizza man also obtained an ankle holster to carry the gun. Just like 007 Agent Bond!

On a midnight shift, a burglar alarm went off at the pizza business. I arrived and saw that all the lights were on in the business. Also, the owner was inside, and the front door was still unlocked.

He seemed to be looking around, and everything looked alright from the outside. I walked in the front door and approached him. I thought he would be expecting the police, and I would normally not surprise a normal, mentally balanced individual. I was dressed in a deputy's uniform with the words "Sheriff's Department" on the shoulder of the sleeves. Also, a five-star badge pinned on my chest. A burglar usually wears dark clothing and may have long hair.

Anyway, he must have been in deep thought as he would imagine maybe someone jumping out at him. I did not see the gun in his hand. I walked up and said, "Any break in?" He turned to me and placed the gun at my chest. I thought he was going to pull the trigger. I had my bulletproof vest on so my plan was to shoot back if he did.

He had a crazed look on his face, and he finally came to his senses. He then began to use his high mental ability to distinguish me as a deputy and not a "green light." He lowered his weapon, and I told him that if I hadn't recognized him as the owner, I would have shot him and been justified. He should have waited for police before entering the business. I told him that a pizza business was not worth getting shot over. He informed me that it was worth it in order to protect it. I guess he felt that the burglars would be able to get away with a lot of dough! After that night, when his alarm went off, I refused to enter his business but merely waited out in the parking lot entrance. I informed my supervisor and requested that his permit be revoked.

I don't believe that all people should carry guns. I don't believe FBI agents should carry guns either.

This should be left for the professionals. I don't want to discuss FBI agents at this point, but let's just say I've worked around them and leave it at that. A cell phone with 911 will suffice. Wait for someone who knows what they're doing. Then hold back and try to remain calm.

CHAPTER 14

———◇◈◇———

Always Write Good Reports

Police have to always write clear, consistent, complete police reports. If one tries to fudge a report, it is a misdemeanor, and one can be arrested. Also, one may have to testify many years later in a court of law.

This happened to me twenty-six years later! I had to testify at fifty-two years of age. I had taken the report at twenty-six years of age. I am glad that I completed a good report and that it helped convict this man of homicide.

It had been a very hot day in the high desert. I was on dayshift and working patrol in the city of Hesperia.

I received a call of a naked woman who was standing by a house with a blanket now wrapped around her.

I responded to the reporting party. The home owner stated that a naked woman, who was only wearing tennis shoes, was upset and knocking on her door. She said she had been sexually assaulted and ran to the nearest house for police.

She said she had met with a man in order to sell him marijuana. She had driven to the back of a liquor store and awaited him. The man eventually drove up in his own car and met with her. The man parked and got into her car for the transaction. The man insisted that they drive off into the desert so he could sample the weed before purchasing. I bet you can already tell what's going to happen.

When they were far enough into the desert, the man asked her to pull off to the side. He then produced a gun. He ordered her to take off her clothes. He allowed her to keep her tennis shoes on because the sand can become quite hot. I have to tell you what he did to a certain point without too much detail, because I would be questioned in court twenty-six years later.

The victim said that he licked one of her breasts and removed his pants. The problem at this point was the twenty-six-year-old man was having problems with a male problem associated with older males twice his age. The erection was just not happening. Almost as embarrassing was the suspect had allowed the female the use of her running shoes. Guess what? He found out that a naked female who's terrified can run very fast with tennis shoes. The suspect fired one shot at the blurred female, who was now picking up more speed. The victim ran to the nearest house to have the owner call the sheriff's office. The suspect drove off with the victim's car and her weed.

I asked the victim the location of the suspect's car, which had been parked behind High Desert Liquor on Main Street in Hesperia. I radioed for a deputy to try to apprehend the suspect who would be trying to get back to his own car.

Deputy Bamley found the suspect at his car and made the arrest. The suspect served time in prison for his crime. I had made sure that a complete report was made on this serious crime.

I was twenty-six at the time, and the suspect was also twenty-six years of age.

Twenty-six years later, I was now fifty-two years old. At fifty-two, I was now employed by San Jose police and had three years to retirement. I was living four hundred miles north of the desert city of Hesperia. I received a phone call from a district attorney investigator in the city of San Gabriel, a suburb of Los Angeles. He was quite surprised that he had found me. I told him that I was now working for San Jose police.

He stated that he needed me to testify as to what had happened twenty-six years ago. He said that the suspect had continued to kidnap women and had graduated to actually killing one of them.

The DA wanted to show that this suspect needed the death penalty. He was a lost cause who would never change. I explained that he would need to send my subpoena to San Jose police.

The county would pay for my airline fare and hotel and meal expenses.

I flew to the Los Angeles area and a DA investigator picked me up at the airport and drove me directly to the court house. Prior to this, the investigator had mailed me a copy of my police report of twenty-six years prior. I was amazed at the neatness of my report and glad I had good writing skills. The investigator was able to find the original victim and Bamley, who was no longer in law enforcement, and also Detective Niller, who did the follow up on the case.

It was like an old family reunion.

I took the stand and explained what had happened twenty-six years prior. The suspect, now grey haired and looking very old, slouched next to his lawyer. I explained what had happened on the day in question.

On cross examination, the defense attorney wanted to know if his client licked the left breast or the right breast of the victim! I testified that I did not remember and did not list it in my report. I explained that I needed to quickly get a deputy to the liquor store to apprehend his client. I had taken a preliminary report and the detective could later be more specific.

Can you believe it? If that was so important to the sick mind of the attorney, he could have asked his client who was seated right next to him! I wanted to ask the defendant in court so his attorney's imagination could be satisfied, but I restrained myself.

I was dismissed a few minutes later. Upon walking out, I stopped and slowly turned, looking at the defendant. The defendant had turned backwards to see me. We both gave each other a look. The defendant immediately looked away and drooped his head in shame. Juries like that emotional action where both officer and defendant give that look to each other. The look was as if we were communicating to each other. I was saying, *I got you now even after twenty-six years.*

I was driven back to a hotel and given a few hundred dollars for meals and a return plane ticket for San Jose. I stayed at the hotel a few days as I liked the swimming pool, and the beer was cold.

I later received a phone call from the DA investigator, who announced that the jury had found the defendant guilty in thirty minutes! A record time for a murder conviction! The investigator announced that his office would send a commendation of me to the chief of police. Ten years later I'm still waiting for that commendation.

If one gets into police work, remember to always write good reports.

CHAPTER 15

———— ◈◈◈ ————

So You Want to Work in Law Enforcement? Plan on Meeting Crazy People

It was a cold, Thanksgiving Day in November. I was working the day shift in Hesperia. The high desert gets quite cold in the winter. The nights can go in the 20s. One can even occasionally have a light snow fall which lasts a day or two. My shift was getting ready to end, and I was looking forward to driving to my parent's house in West Covina for the Thanksgiving meal.

I was hoping that everyone would behave so I wouldn't get any calls. Nope. "5 Paul 6, Victorville." I answered back, "Paul 6." "Possible intoxicated male at the High Desert Apartments, yelling, and he may be injured." "Paul 6 en route."

Great! Here comes the drunk idiots, and it's not even four p.m. I responded and located a man walking around and yelling. I stopped him and had him come over to my patrol car. His right hand was bleeding.

I couldn't wait to hear his story. Why do some people make life so hard for themselves? He explained that he got into an argument with another man who had held a knife at him. The man had held the knife out at about chest height with the blade pointing upward. This guy grabbed the knife by the blade, stating, "Don't pull a knife at me!" They then had a brief arm wrestling-type match which the drunk actually won. The only problem was that he had been holding the blade part. His hand was now significantly bleeding and would need stiches in the least.

I placed him under arrest for public intoxication and drove him to Victorville Desert Hospital. The doctor examined his hand and said he would have to go into surgery. Soon, the sergeant showed up at the hospital and asked me why I had arrested him. I told the good sergeant that he could not care for his own safety due to intoxication and might have later got himself shot or killed. I was expecting a "Oh, good job!" Instead the sergeant went through his sour face making, which was very theatrical. This sergeant also had an alcohol problem, so maybe he felt bad for the fellow drunk. I could only guess.

Anyway, the sergeant explained that the county would be liable for surgery payment as he was in my custody. I asked what I should do. The doctor had advised that he would need to go down to the San Bernardino hospital to be treated by a hand specialist.

The good sergeant told me to unarrest him and give him a courtesy ride down to San Bernardino.

I was then to drop him off at the front entrance of the hospital and encourage him to go inside to be seen by their doctor. I had the Victorville doctor bandage his hand in order to transport him.

I told the inmate that I and the sergeant had felt so sorry for him that I was releasing him from my custody and would still give him a free ride to San Bernardino. He was more than delighted.

I dropped him off at the front entrance, and by the time he found out that he was duped, I would be halfway back to Victorville and forty miles away. I felt sorry for the San Bernardino central deputies, but things like this do happen.

If you ever feel inclined to wrestle with a knife from someone, don't grab the blade end!

*****

Ever wonder what a crazy, naked man does with a banana? Why, he crushes it between his toes!

Just in case you see this question on a test.

I was working day shift in Apple Valley. This was where the late Roy Rogers lived. I responded to an expensive home in regards to a naked man seen walking inside his house. By this time, nothing was surprising me anymore. You see, the desert was getting to me. I was now of same character and mind as the "desert folk." I thought, *So, what, the guy was going outside, maybe to get the paper, and he forgot to put his robe on.*

I arrived and saw that the front door was open and the drapes were blowing from the desert wind.

It looked like the start of an Alfred Hitchcock thriller movie. If I could just hear the spooky music start to play, then the scene would be complete. I went inside alone, because I didn't have backup.

I noticed a naked man looking at me, and I asked if he was okay. He appeared to be in his fifties but was still in combative shape if it came to that. Now, on a call like this, one has to talk more and go into action less. I radioed Victorville substation and asked for backup. The nearest unit was in a private community about twenty-five miles away! Okay, I had about twenty minutes to socialize with this nut case. I thought about tackling him and forcing him into cuffs, but the thought of wrestling with a naked crazy guy didn't appeal to me at the time. So I would wait for backup and maybe learn an interesting story from this guy.

I learned that he was an engineer by trade, which would explain the expensive house. He probably went off his medication, so this would explain the absence of a wife or girlfriend. He showed me some porno magazines and said that this was what he truly needed. So that had answered my first question.

We walked into the kitchen area, and he showed me how he could squish a banana between his toes. I stayed with him to make sure he didn't grab a knife or weapon to use on me. Did I mention that twenty minutes seemed like eternity when you're waiting for someone, mainly another deputy?

Finally, Deputy Lew arrived, and we each grabbed a wrist and placed him in handcuffs. We allowed him to get clothing for his new date with ward B, located in San Bernardino. We had a forty-five-minute drive together down the Cajon Pass and into the beautiful smog-filled sky of San Bernardino.

*****

On the weekends in the high desert, people come out to enjoy the openness of the desert. Some come to ride motorcycles on the El Mirage dry lake. Others come to shoot rifles, even though it's illegal to shoot a weapon other than a shotgun. The shotgun's pellets don't travel as far as a bullet, so it's a lot safer from that perspective.

One father was riding a motorcycle, with his son on a smaller motorcycle. They were having a good time. Somehow, the father fell backwards, and his son stopped to see why. He was bleeding from the face and no longer moving. The son went for help. Nearby dirt bike riders came up and saw that there was a hole where the man's eye used to be. The sheriff's department was called, and I received the call to respond a few miles out onto the dry lake. Also, a sheriff's helicopter was en route as my backup.

I noted that the man had been shot right through his goggles and into his eye. It looked as if a sniper had shot him with pinpoint accuracy. Witnesses pointed to a large group of people about three hundred yards away and noticed that they had been shooting a rifle.

The helicopter landed with more deputies. We made contact with the group. We learned that a father was allowing his twelve-year-old daughter to shoot a rifle at a target with no background to stop a bullet, which can travel over one mile! The motorcyclist was right in the line of fire. The father was too stupid and without common sense to supervise his daughter. The coroner arrived and took over the deceased and the investigation. The man was cited, and the report was submitted to the district attorney for criminal charges. The girl was cited into juvenile probation for review.

Many preventable accidents happen in the desert on the weekends such as this one. Sometimes, people don't think!

*****

There are gold miners out here in the desert! Actually, they mine in the mountains on the backside of the San Bernardino mountain range. And they are also crazy! They drink heavily and get into arguments. They have rifles and guns to protect their claims.

On this warm winter day, I would meet with one who needed to report a possible murder.

"Paul 7, Victorville!" I responded, "Victorville, go!" "Paul 7, meet the man at Bear Valley Road and Apple Valley Road in regards to a possible shooting." "Paul 7 copy," I responded.

I met with Robert Whitman at the location. Robert stated that he lives in a mining camp up in the mountains with several other men. He went on to say that they share a claim on the backside of the mountains. Last night, Robert got into an argument with another man. They live in their own individual trailers on site. Each man has a shotgun for protection.

Robert said that it had been pitch black during the night. The men argued, and the possible victim went back to his trailer to retrieve his shotgun. The man shot at Robert but missed. Being a sensible crazy person, Robert grabbed his shotgun and aimed at the darkness, where he felt the man might be standing. He cautiously pulled back on the trigger and heard the loud boom!

In the darkness, Robert heard, "Oh, you got me!" Frightened, Robert ran for his car and began driving down the mountainous road, because this is what crazy people do after they shoot someone.

Wow! I thought, this is something you don't see every day! It's people like Robert who make law enforcement so interesting. Can you imagine how boring the job would be if one just got up in the morning and went to work and paid taxes?

Robert was about fifty years old and looked like he might travel with a mule. He had gray hair and a beard. I was disappointed to learn that he drove a car but not when reporting a possible homicide, because his driver's license was suspended. I just thought he would look cool with a mule in tow.

I grew up watching *Bonanza* on Sunday night, and that was how gold miners traveled.

I had to handle this call by myself. There just were not any units to assist me. As I look back, I could have been ambushed by a crazy guy who needed a patrol car. But after meeting little miss house coat with a shotgun and a guy wrapped in explosives, Robert seemed quite safe. I had also survived the Alamo attack, and I was feeling quite confident in myself. In truth, I think the desert sun had baked my brains and I was becoming just as crazy as my clients. After remembering Mr. Pizza with a hand gun, I made sure that Robert did not have any weapons on him.

We drove up 3N14, which is a forestry dirt road that leaves Apple Valley and heads up into the backside of the beautiful pine covered mountains of San Bernardino. It is a pleasant, slow, and bumpy ride, and one gains elevation quite rapidly. And with a crazy man sitting next to me, I could not ask for better company and conversation. I let Robert ride in the front seat as he was such a pleasant individual, and I thought that it would be special for him to later tell his friends that he had ridden in the front seat of a patrol car as opposed to the back seat in handcuffs.

As we drove up the mountain side, Robert explained that men like him will find old mines and start working them with other men. No one gets paid, and when and if they find gold, they split the earnings evenly. When the men are not finding any treasure, tempers can flare up and fights break out. Robert feared that we would find a dead coworker on the ground when we arrived. If that was the case, Robert would be dining in the Victorville jail with a TV dinner on the menu. I think miners only eat pork and beans, so maybe a TV dinner was not that bad.

We drove for about forty-five minutes and maybe an hour at approximately twenty mph. The air conditioner on the underpowered patrol car growled in protest, and it blew air onto us. The county always buys the cheapest cars at fleet prices at a great discount. The Ford Fairmont kept climbing, and I was glad the county did not purchase any Ford Pintos, because they could have saved even more money. For those too young to know what a Ford Pinto is, just envision a really crappy car.

We arrived at the possible crime scene, and I noted several trailers parked close to each other. I climbed out with the shotgun in the low ready position and racked a shell in the chamber.

Robert showed me where he had been standing and where the victim would have fallen. There was no body and no evidence of blood or of a body being dragged away. The crazy man had tricked Robert into thinking he had been shot. Just a couple of miners having a good time.

No one else was around, and I was interested in seeing an actual mine and how it worked. I replaced the shotgun in the car and walked over to the entrance of the mine. Robert started up a generator, and a series of lights went on in the mine tunnel. I followed Robert into the mine and only got about fifty yards inside when I discovered that I have claustrophobia. Great! First, I find out that I can be hypnotized very easily, and now, I have claustrophobia! I'm sorry to say that I can never be a miner.

I guess I'll just have to remain working for a living.

I retreated out and thought that the sunshine never felt so good. As we drove back down the mountain, Robert explained that when they hit a vein upon striking with a hammer and pick, the rock would shimmer in a sparkly color. The feeling was glorious and kept miners engaged in their endeavor, even when finding out later that it was just a worthless mineral.

I was then able to tell Robert a story of gold seekers. I explained that people travel on the freeway, passing right through Victorville. They arrive in Las Vegas with the hope of striking it big. A few can spend a certain amount of money and then go home, remembering that they had a good time and did not break the bank. Others cannot. They are addicted, and they cannot stop. They continue to gamble and lose everything. Once they find out they don't have gas money, they go into pawnshops and sell their watches and rings for money and continue to gamble. When this is gone, I assume they beg for gas money to get home. With only five dollars of gas, they begin to travel home. The car runs out of gas around the area of Victorville. They feel so stupid and need more gas money. They then walk into the Victorville sheriff's substation, and instead of saying they're stupid and need money to get home, they invent a story of themselves being robbed and their watches and rings got stolen.

I have seen this happen several times. They think they have come up with the ultimate story to avoid having to say they're stupid. I remember telling one taxpayer that reporting a false report is a crime. Also, I was getting tired of writing false police reports so he could face his wife when he got home. In fact, I told several people that we would give them a five-dollar gas voucher and that this would get them into San Bernardino. I advised them to not try to make up false reports and to just tell the police that they needed help getting home. I noted that many people are not honest with themselves. They think they are clever and cunning, but I did not intend to write about the Clintons. They come in all tax brackets.

Some become president, but all are still who they are, not what they think they are.

Robert was stunned! He could not believe that people could be this dishonest! Compared to the people I explained to Robert, he felt that maybe he was not such a bad guy after all. At least he was honest about shooting at someone. How could anyone be so deceitful!

I dropped Robert off near his car and wished him good luck. I completed a report of my investigation.

It's good to meet honest people in law enforcement from time to time.

*****

Search and Rescue

One of the things that I missed about the sheriff's department was the fact that they conducted lots of search and rescues. We had a sheriff's mounted unit consisting of reserve deputies on horseback. We also had a jeep unit which could scour the desert for lost people. Then there was a mine recovery unit. Yes, we have numerous mines throughout the desert! On one incident, a dirt bike rider drove/fell into a mine, landing fifty feet to the bottom. The mine recovery team consisted of rope experts and mountain climbers who could go into the mine and help the injured to safety. On the mountains, there were mountain climbing experts. In the waterways, there was a rescue scuba team used mostly for life saving and body recovery. We had a fleet of helicopters. Some were used for air patrol, and others for medevacs. The pilots were mostly from the Vietnam era, so they were wild when pursuing a vehicle or getting to a deputy who needed backup.

If you were watching the news in 2015, you may have heard of and seen the incident where San Bernardino deputies in Hesperia were chasing a man from his car and, later, from a stolen horse! The video shows the deputies finally stopping the man and appear to rough him up—all caught on camera by a news helicopter. This pursuit started in Victorville and in an attempt to serve a warrant at a home. The parolee with a violent background jumped into a car and was pursued into the foothills of Hesperia. He came to a dead-end and ran. He found a man sunbathing near Deep Creek with a horse waiting nearby. Deep Creek is known for nude sunbathers. The suspect then headed off into the sunset. The deputies continued on foot. A sheriff's helicopter began to drop deputies off in a wide perimeter in order to surround the suspect, which they finally did. The suspect resisted the entire time until taken into custody. Two deputies suffered dehydration, with one almost passing out. They needed to be airlifted out. These men and women gave it their all and, when faced with a difficult job, performed admirably. I recently read that the deputies faced hung juries, and the DA offered them a plea bargain down to PC 415, misdemeanor disturbance, which they accepted, dropping the felony charges they were facing.

I was working in the Wild West, and it had been interesting. In eight years, I could write an entire book on my adventures, but there was something missing; namely, a good salary. Remember the Wonder Bread driver and deliverer who was making one dollar more than me? No, I wasn't about to start driving a delivery van.

CHAPTER 16

———◇◈◇———

Lord, Show Me Where! I will follow

In 1983, I found myself married to my first wife. I felt that it was the right thing to do. I did not ask the Lord for his opinion. I did not seek advice from anyone. I didn't need advice. When one marries, they simply live happy ever after. Police have a problem of being white knights. They can solve any problem and make things right. Wrong. Here comes another life lesson.

This is why some police officers are married several times, yet they're still divorced or unhappy. And the ones who remain married, they probably can't afford a divorce, so they just sweat it out and cope. Anyway, more about this later in the book.

My then wife and I had a son. I never thought I would be so excited to be a dad. It was a miracle. He was handed to me, and I swear I was walking at least one foot off the ground. I looked into his eyes and saw Jesus looking right back at me. I couldn't believe the love I felt for him. I never felt love in this power, and it made me think of what love the Lord has for me. I never even liked kids before this.

I used to see kids waving at me from their parent's cars and really didn't want to wave back. Now, after that, if I see a kid in a car seat, I would initiate the wave with a comical smile on my face. I could see him telling his mom about what just occurred. She would look at me to smile, but I would look straight ahead and not make eye contact as if nothing had happened. I could see the kid explain,

"Mom, I'm not kidding. He was waving at me!" You see, I didn't realize how special these miracles really were.

I was now seeing life in a different, more serious way. We joined a church and became Baptists.

I was beginning to pray more about life and for general direction in life. Also, something else was missing: a decent salary where I made more than the Wonder Bread delivery driver.

With a bachelor's degree in criminology, I felt there was more. At thirty years of age, I took two classes at law school. I enrolled in a class of agency and a class of community property, which discussed divorce and division of property. Little did I know that I would write and testify to my very own divorce, about ten years and several months later, as *pro per*, which is basically an acting attorney. I was hoping to make myself attractive for an opportunity as an FBI agent or a deputy DA.

I finished one semester with average grades and felt that law school was not for me. I also looked at the bulletin board and saw many applicants trying to get jobs as attorneys. Apparently, even after one passes the bar, one still has to look hard for a job. Starting your own law firm is hard with no experience. A deputy DA has a fully overloaded case load with no time for presentation of a crime.

When I applied for the FBI, I traveled to Los Angeles to take what the government calls a "test."

It's more like a game where they ask you questions about how you were raised, what your favorite color is, etc. The written test goes on from there, asking about a full page of long vocabulary words. These long words are never used in interviews or testifying, because no one will understand what one is saying. Authors like using long unknown words in their books to demonstrate and impress the reader with their mature use of the English language. In other words, the government found some pencil neck to write up an exam to determine if one is capable of becoming an FBI agent.

I took the exam three different times, and each time, I received a card in the mail stating that my grades were not competitive. I later learned that the FBI was fishing for lawyers, accountants, and females. I was none of these.

Have you ever prayed for something and did not get it? Then later you found out that it was something that you were grateful for not obtaining? If ever you attend a class reunion and there was a cute girl who you never had the nerve to ask out on a date. Then at the reunion, you saw her, and she had apparently had let her looks go. Maybe Jenny Craig was not called into the problem in time. Or maybe as a girl, you saw the star of the football team, and now he resembles Homer Simpson. Anyway, that's what the FBI turned out to be for me. Thank you, Lord, for unanswered prayers.

I had kept seeing a hiring poster for San Jose police. The pay was outstanding! I could make more money than I would have working for the FBI or the district attorney's office! But I would put this into prayer and follow where God wanted me to be. I noted that they required one to have at least sixty units of college experience. I have always felt that police should have some degree of college work behind them. With the sheriff's department, I was actually working with some people who only had a GED education! Many deputies were obtaining bachelor's degrees later as the job was getting more competitive. I actually had a sergeant with a GED education write my evaluation report and put in that I was low in my education requirement! He said I would need to take law enforcement courses during the year to bring up my status! When a supervisor with a GED and an alcohol problem tells you that you are low in education, and the Wonder Bread driver passes you on the way home, it's time to look for another job.

Did you realize that God appoints people to become police officers? The ones who are not appointed can usually be read about in a newspaper, and it is always negative. Also, when God has a calling in someone's life, not only will doors open for you, but when you stray away, you'll be pulled back into the calling.

I was not allowed to leave law enforcement, but I was about to embark on a great journey and meet some of the best officers in the country. As I look back, I'm glad that God was pushing and I was going.

I phoned San Jose police personnel and was given a written test date. I was told to order a book and study it. It was not about vocabulary or how I was raised as a child. It was about police work and investigation. I arrived in San Jose and took the test on a Saturday. It was great to be in the cool, coastal air of the Bay Area. I looked at the test questions and saw immediately that something was wrong. All the questions pertained to the book I had studied. I passed with flying colors. These guys were more intelligent than the FBI and their testing procedures. I actually learned later that the test was hard for some people who didn't pass.

I worried over the psychology testing, afraid that the desert sun had indeed baked my brains and that I would fail. To my surprise, I tested to be a mentally balanced individual who was capable of the stress of law enforcement who would never let alcohol or drugs or excuses rule my life. One who could maintain a good balance in both personal as well as employment life in a mature and unbiased manner. One who could—okay, I made that part up. But I did pass.

The physical was easy. One had to run a mile; I believe it was ten minutes. Jump a six-foot wall and drag a heavy bag a certain distance. Very easy, but I was astounded to see some individuals not pass the running. If you can't run one mile in ten minutes, why are you wasting your time here?

We were notified that this would have to be accomplished before testing!

Next came the back Xray. Did you know that fifty percent fail and don't realize they have a bad back that will later cause themselves problems? Anyway, I passed, so I am grateful for a strong back.

The background test is a test that you can't study for. You either have a good background or you don't. If you lie about yourself, it will come out later. Bill Clinton or Hillary would never make this test. Their integrity would not allow it.

I had a background investigator drive to Victorville to conduct my background. My sweet and unbiased captain said that I was okay, but I always felt that I deserved better than the sheriff's department.

Upon learning that I was trying to get hired by an outside department, He placed me back on the midnight shift. The only thing close to a union was SEBA, and they had no bite. What had I got myself into? I was now on a s--- list.

Two weeks later, I received a phone call asking if I still wanted the job. Yes! Goodbye, Captain!

Finally, a decent paycheck, and they have a very strong police union. Also, they have backup when one is needed.

*****

Slave to sin, Paul writes to the Romans in the Bible:

Why is it that what I want to do, I do not
do. Yet, what I do not want to do, I do?
—Romans 7:14–25

Why do men and women in a position of trust wind up disappointing us at times? Whether it is a spouse, a police officer, a judge, a priest, or a politician?

"Paul 2, Victorville." I responded, "Paul 2." "Shoplifter at Kmart on 7th St." "Paul 2 copy." I thought, *Well, another kid caught shoplifting.*

Bill Bright was a fifty-one-year-old juvenile probation officer. He dressed sharp with a suit and a gold watch and ring. All my juvenile crime reports were referred to him and the juvenile court.

I entered the Kmart and was shown to a rear office where the store security office was. Wow, Bill was already there to take this juvenile away. Only, where was the juvenile? "Hey, Bill, where's the juvenile?" He only looked down at his shoes, stating, "I just wanted to see if it was as easy as some of my kids were saying it was, you know, to shoplift." I responded, "Oh, I guess you let the store manager know that you were only testing and not really stealing, right?"

The store detective then said, "No, he actually stole a musical cassette tape!" Bill replied, "But I fully intended to return it!" I asked the store security where he had been detained. He replied that he had followed him out to his car and stopped him. He had no intention of returning it.

Acting Senior Deputy Smith arrived and told me that he worked things out with the manager and that Bill would be free to go. I advised that I preferred to book Bill into custody and could cite release him with a court date. I wasn't about to let any crook go. Bill looked just as good sitting in the back of my patrol car as anyone else as we embarked on our journey to the slammer.

I submitted my report to the district attorney's office. The district attorney's office is located right next to the juvenile probation's office. The DA wanted to know why I didn't think Bill would return the tape and wanted a supplemental report before he would file. I recontacted the security who stated that Bill had removed the cellophane tape around the cassette prior to attempting to get in his car. The store cannot resell the tape at this time.

I forwarded my report, and Bill was convicted. He also got a one-month suspension from work.

An employee who works at juvenile probation can walk into the sheriff's substation and walk directly into the rear locker room area of the deputies. About a week later, this is exactly what Bill did. He approached me at my locker and thanked me for being so professional and polite to him. I told Bill that he was fifty-one years old and had no business doing anything so stupid. It would be foolish to throw away employment at any age, let alone fifty-one years. I explained that a deputy would lose his job completely over a theft. Bill thanked me again and left the locker room.

During the course of my employment, I have arrested numerous shoplifters that were way past adolescent age. Guess what? This was not the first time Bill had stolen anything. I believe that this was only the first time Bill was caught! Most store detectives will not watch a fifty-one-year old man dressed in a suit with a gold wrist watch. But that day had been different for Bill. He was watched, and the arriving deputy was there to do God's work. Book him!

Kleptomania is a serious illness that leads to behavior similar to Bill's. I believe the person feels that something is owed to him or her. It's a feeling of entitlement much similar to what a democrat feels but much stronger. It's the excitement of knowing you got away with something much like Bill Clinton felt with Monica, for a while at least.

CHAPTER 17

─────◆◆◆◆─────

When Deputies and Police Officers Become Inmates

She was fifteen years old with a pimpled face and had an attraction to law enforcement officers. Worse, she was an explorer scout with the sheriff's department. Our job was to allow her to ride on patrol with deputies who would ensure her safety and not try to take advantage of a curious, youthful, and highly confused teenager.

She rode with me on a few patrol shifts. I could tell that she was probably available and could easily flirt and use poor judgment around much older men. I was recently married and promised to keep my marriage vows. Also, I had no desire to intimidate a confused teenager for my own selfish sexual desires. Also, I believe I am watched from above at all times.

I had heard rumors that she had been seeing the jail deputy, which was a new position, so the jail would no longer have to be manned by street patrol deputies. These correction deputies were not qualified to patrol or carry guns.

While she rode on patrol with me, I tried to give her counseling much like a big brother would to a confused little sister. The jailor was much older and happened to be married. I thought that she only had a crush on the jailor, nothing more. I tried to reason with her to date only boys that were her same age with her parent's approval of course. I would later learn that the problem was much more serious. I felt that she and her behavior would still be safe because she was around law enforcement professionals who were sworn for her safety. Boy, was I wrong!

Apparently, there had been an office party which I did not attend. It had gotten wild, and I do mean *wild*. The captain's desk had been used in a manner that was not appropriate with a deputy and a dispatcher who were both married to different spouses. I'm sure the captain had the desk washed numerous times after, but the thought alone would cause one to request a different desk.

Then came even more bad news. The explorer scout was now claiming that she was a victim of oversexed deputies and had been present at the office party.

This couldn't be real! We worked so hard to be deputies. These men wouldn't risk their careers for a pimple-faced youth. A few of the deputies had very attractive wives. It didn't make sense.

The explorer had to be lying, I thought.

One deputy was brought into the station. After being interviewed, he was walked back into the jail and booked for rape of an underaged girl. The next deputy was brought in for questioning. When he came in, I asked him if the charges were true. He looked at me and said that the explorer scout was a liar. Wow. This was a deputy who I had gone with on many calls for service!

I went home and explained to my then wife that I would probably be called in and falsely accused of rape as they were taking the word of a juvenile. I thought that she must be lying as these deputies were men of honor. I had the explorer scout ride with me on several occasions.

Guess what! I never got that call. I would later read in the Victorville News of several deputies being arrested and their pending court dates in the future. The explorer had been telling the truth. I guess I would have to patrol the streets of Victorville, Hesperia, and Apple Valley alone with no backup. Maybe this would be a good time to ask for a raise?

Not to worry, I received my acceptance for employment with San Jose police. I would receive a huge raise. The morale was down, and people in the community were not showing trust toward the sheriff's department over a few dishonest deputies.

I want to add that these were only a few of the bad apples. The sheriff's department as a majority has many trustworthy deputies who put their lives on the line every day. It had been an honor working with these fine men and women for almost eight years. The San Bernardino sheriff's department has fabulous training courses in pursuit driving and officer survival. Departments from all over the country pay to have their officers travel and attend their courses in San Bernardino that can last up to several days.

A part of me will always be a San Bernardino deputy in my heart. On my last day, I received a plaque which stated: "Thanks for an outstanding job, from your fellow workers of the Victorville substation."

Below the plaque was a baton. I'm glad it had not been a six-celled metal flashlight. Can you imagine!

I had to leave this place before anyone said anything good about me. You could have knocked me over with a feather! But I was in search of a cooler, coastal climate, and I had heard too many great things about one of the finest police departments in the country.

The song "Do You Know the Way to San Jose" kept playing in my sun-baked mind as I exited the substation parking lot for the last time. I would miss the crazy people of the high desert who gave me great job security in a hot and dusty environment.

CHAPTER 18

———◇◈◇———

San Jose Police Department

M y hiring date was May 18, 1986. I had moved my one-year-old son and first wife four hundred miles north of San Bernardino. We rented a house in Livermore, about thirty miles north of San Jose. I had two weeks from separation of employment of the San Bernardino sheriff's department and then swearing in at San Jose police. I was a civilian for two weeks, and it was a good feeling being sworn back in as a law enforcement officer again.

I could feel the coastal breeze of the San Francisco Bay and welcomed its cool relief. I would experience my first summer without heat, which could reach 107 degrees back in the desert. An officer must always wear a bulletproof vest, which makes the heat that much harder to bear. The traffic leading into San Jose was terrible. It was times like this when I regretted leaving the high desert.

Another thing that was different was that the CHP Officers were very young and mostly in their 20s.

San Jose police were older officers and could be twice their age. I found out that when CHP officers got released from the academy, they had to start their careers in large cities. Only with seniority were they able to move out to rural areas, much like Victorville. The police in San Jose were not as close to CHP as we had been as deputies in a rural area. I relied on CHP backup many times in Victorville as they could be the closest backup to my location.

Another difference with San Jose is that the police department is much larger than the county sheriff. In Los Angeles, the sheriff's department is larger than the Los Angeles police. All surrounding police agencies were jealous of our paychecks. The Wonder Bread drivers made far less than police.

I was quite glad that the FBI had not hired me. I was making more money, and I would not have to worry about being sent to North Dakota to investigate Indian rights violations. One female officer had quit San Jose police to join the FBI, and that is exactly what Uncle Sam did to her! She was used to the high training standards of San Jose and could not believe the poor safety tactics of federal investigators. They only look good in the movies, but in real life, it's quite embarrassing. Anyway, she gladly returned to San Jose and got her job back. Another life experience learned the hard way.

My first week at San Jose included an in-house orientation to the department. I was joined by three other "laterals" from different agencies. A lateral is a deputy or officer who has already passed through a police or sheriff's academy which cost that department over $10,000 as of 1986 and probably three times as much in today's economy. Most have also passed through their one-year probation and are competent street officers. There is almost no risk as they also will have a good evaluation from their previous employment. San Jose police save thousands of dollars by hiring laterals. Imagine a lot of officers who pass the academy and then fail at the field training program or, after a few years, cannot cope with stress of police work. Many thousands of dollars in training wasted, or worse, the officer is involved in a criminal matter or "bad shooting," which costs the city several million in punitive damages.

There are three levels of postcertificates for peace officers. The basic post is completion of an academy and one-year police service. Next is the intermediate post. This is four years in law enforcement with an AA degree or two years in law enforcement and a BA degree. Finally, there is the advanced post, where one has to have nine years in law enforcement and an AA degree or six years in law enforcement with a BA degree or four years in law enforcement with a MA degree.

I came to San Jose with an advanced postcertificate, quite a savings for San Jose and a fantastic employment opportunity for me. I found out that there were many officers with master's degrees.

A few with doctor's degrees and several who were attorneys. This was a very educated police department. This was a long way from a former sheriff sergeant with a GED education who gave me an evaluation with a "Needs Education" on my yearly evaluation report.

It was great to see that law enforcement was attracting and requiring members to have college education backgrounds. Departments were now paying enough to recruit some of the best in the country.

I started my San Jose career with a week-long program called "in-house." The four lateral officers started with a graduating academy class from Evergreen Academy. This academy seemed nothing like my San Bernardino stress academy had been. Two of the people of this academy would later become police chiefs. These were truly smart officers who were designed for competition.

We had in-house classes showing us the many different units of the department—street crimes, merge (which is their word for SWAT), vice, narcotics, motorcycles, missing persons, homicide, sexual assault, and many more. My favorite buddies, internal affairs, and then we heard from our police union. What a strong union! This, I was not used to. The union president told us that we were not to go into any IA investigation without a union representative. We actually had rights! If we were to call in sick and we were later asked where our location of sickness was, we were to tell them that it was not any of their business!

San Bernardino never had a strong union like this. These people knew what the law was.

We had attorneys standing by, appointed by the union if needed. They were paid for by union fees.

Finally, crooks weren't the only ones who had rights. We had rights too! I didn't have to worry about being hypnotized or interviewed by some selfish sergeant who merely wanted to be promoted to lieutenant and cared less about my career.

After in-house training, we were assigned to a field training officer. Oh, no! Not another FTO!

The last one almost killed me! To my surprise, these guys were actually here to help me evolve and become acclimated to the San Jose police environment. One actually helped me carry my equipment to my locker! We would be assigned a different FTO every four weeks. After three FTOs passed us, we could move on to going solo in a car. Wow! My very own car! By myself!

I noticed that we had many different races and people from all backgrounds on this department.

San Jose has a large population of Hispanics, Vietnamese, Chinese, East Indians, Cambodians, Japanese, African Americans. And now they had me, and I was actually born in Canada.

When I began driving around my beat in San Jose, I noticed that the public had a deep respect for officers. When someone was asked to remain at a car or submit to a pat down search, they complied. The few times that they ran, there were so many patrol units that showed up in a few minutes that it would overwhelm me. Usually, there could be a helicopter overhead and a K9 officer present. Once, I had a motorcycle officer chase down a suspect I was running after. Another time I had an undercover officer walk up on a suspect who was hiding from me. The suspect never knew who would be grabbing him.

My first FTO had a problem with me not learning the ten-codes. The ten-codes are not usually used in Southern California. For instance, when stopping a vehicle, the deputy would say, "Control, vehicle stop, Main St. and Vine." With the ten-code, an officer says, "Control, 11-95 Main St. and Vine." After eight years of talking on the radio and speaking plain English, I now had to speak in secret code.

Believe me, with scanners out there, crooks and citizens figure out what an 11-95 is. Someone at this department must have watched too much *Adam-12* on TV while growing up. Bet you already know what a 211 is. The FTO had me making PCP arrests all night long. Then after work, I would have two hours of paperwork, which he got to sit back and collect two hours of overtime at a time-and-a-half pay compensation. He wrote me up for failure to learn the ten-codes in a few weeks. Instead of concentrating on my ten-code techniques, we made PCP influence arrests. I later found out that he was hired for his Spanish speaking abilities and did not have a full sixty units for qualifications for employment. He had to promise to eventually gain his college units.

My next FTO was a lateral from the Santa Clara county sheriff's department. We went on several disturbance calls, which he felt were handled remarkably well. I explained that in the desert, I had to handle crazy people, alone, all the time. He was very impressed by my call handling techniques and told me not to worry about ten-codes, as it would come in time. I had a good four weeks with Jack, and he marveled at the fact that we weren't a training unit but a two-man car. Jack had actually graduated from law school but was having trouble passing the Bar exam. In the four weeks with Jack, I was using the ten-codes much better. I was then passed on to my third and last FTO, Don. Don saw that I handled calls well, and he proved to be relaxed and easygoing. I merely had to take interest in his building expertise. Don had his contractor's license and built houses on the side.

At two and a half months, I had passed through the FTO program and was now able to ride solo in my own patrol car. Now, all I had to worry was getting through my one-year long probation period, and I could be considered as a reliable full-time employee and officer.

The uniforms were dark blue with a white stripe going down the outside length of the pant leg.

I thought it looked pretty awesome. The patrol cars were a midnight blue and looked almost black—much more intimidating than the white cars that the sheriff's department had. And the cars were clean and not beat-up looking. These cars were fast too, just as fast as the CHP's units.

And the air conditioning units actually worked! When I pulled over a vehicle, a second unit would always join me as a "fill unit." Remember, in Southern California, it was known as a "backup," but here in the Bay Area, it's a "fill."

The citizens and noncitizens had a tremendous respect for San Jose police. Even criminals gave tremendous respect for our commands and orders. Many criminals complained that they could commit crimes in San Francisco and Oakland, but as soon as they tried something in San Jose, they would be caught. The district attorney's office stated that San Jose's crime reports were accurate and concise and that they were able to file charges on the majority of police reports. The officers were also noted for testifying in a credible and truthful manner. Los Angeles police do not have this record or level of education. Do you remember the OJ Simpson trial with the lead investigator? Los Angeles only requires a high school degree, and they have been known to actually hire former gang members.

You get what you pay for, and LAPD salary is not worth applying for. Outside of California, the police's salary is even more dismal.

San Jose has a high level of high paying salaries for many citizens, mostly because of Silicon Valley and the computer and technical industries. Many computer geniuses come here to work, bringing in great revenue for the city. Almaden Valley is at the west side of San Jose and has many millionaires living there. On the Eastside of San Jose lies a rougher area, at least in the 1980s. There was actually an apartment complex which had housed individuals who would shoot at patrol vehicles.

Story and King was always exciting with a shooting or stabbing or police pursuit. I was homesick for the Wild West, coming from the high desert and Roy Rogers. But the Eastside filled that void.

I was overcome with gratitude, as police work can become boring without the excitement of the western frontier. I should have learned Spanish, but most of the officers were Spanish speaking and were always available.

On the Westside, I felt like a glorified security guard for the upper class. But here on the Eastside, when someone reported an assault, it usually involved a stabbing or shooting incident. But truthfully, it was the upper class who were paying most of the bills which included my paycheck. I love taxpayers.

San Jose had the best of both worlds. Some officers preferred the Westside, and some preferred the Eastside. Or if one likes crazy people, one could bid for the central, downtown area. Lots of halfway houses for the mentally disturbed individuals who needs group home intervention. When I would see some of these individuals, some resembled zombies, and around Halloween, it could place one in a true Halloween spirit.

We got to work a four-day workweek consisting of a ten-hour shift. With three days off, I became involved in working pay jobs or moonlighting for extra pay. There were always paid security jobs for San Jose police as businesses did not want to hire security guards. Most police had families with small children, and the bills always came in at the end of the month. The harder I worked, the faster my first wife could spend. Many bills were paid with credit cards with high interest rates.

The harder I worked, the unhappier my first wife became. The unhappier she became, the more she spent. My first marriage was a sinking ship that would only stay afloat for a little over ten years. I kept bailing out water, but the hole grew bigger, and the ship would eventually sink.

A funny thing about some marriages. On one's wedding day, they feel as if they are marrying the *Star Wars*'s Princess Leia of their dreams. Six months later, they find out that they are married to Carry Fisher, complete with drug, alcohol, and emotional baggage that would choke a baggage carousel at any airports. Or for the female who believes she's marrying Prince Charming, only to learn one year later that she's married to Homer Simpson.

I'll discuss later in the book how to avoid the above and marry with more success. Many police are married several times and still failing. When you're in a hole, it's important that you stop digging!

Another word of advice: Doing the same thing again and expecting different results is the definition of insanity.

As I mentioned earlier, San Jose has a strong police union. In our ten-hour shift, we were granted a thirty-minute lunch break. If it went to forty minutes, it was understandable. Supervisors made sure one got his lunch or dinner, referred to as "code 7." One was also granted potty breaks, better known as "B-Boy." "Control, I'll be B-Boy at Quimby at White."

I missed tracking suspects as this is impossible in the city. But I could catch many crimes in progress, because I could be only a few blocks away when a crime was occurring. When a crook ran from me, a perimeter could be established in a few minutes from other responding units. Usually, the crook would hide in someone's backyard. A K9 unit would respond, and a yard-to-yard search would occur with the excitement of hearing the K9 barking excitedly and with a good bite or two. Many times, a helicopter hovered overhead in a circular movement. San Jose was indeed a bad place to be a crook.

Before I go on, I want to say that before the K9 was released in a yard, the K9 officer would warn the crook to surrender, because the canine would bite. Several seconds would pass, and the crook could surrender and not get bit, or he could play his cards and find out another life lesson the hard way. Dogs are not stupid, and they will find you! Crooks, unfortunately, are stupid.

*****

San Jose police have several other quality characteristics that make it stand out ahead of other police agencies. I noted that there is less of the Marine/Army attitude and more of a professional business atmosphere. Here, if you have an idea, you can present it to a supervisor or a written statement to the city itself. If it is a good idea, they will actually implement it. If it saves the city money, one can actually get a small cash award. Even as an officer, you're treated as an adult regardless of rank.

While in both sheriffs' departments, if you didn't have rank, you were allowed to keep your mouth shut and follow orders. Ask no questions and bob your head up and down, much like the ceramic dogs that you see on the back of a vehicle shelf with a spring neck that bobbed up and down while driving down the street. I'm sure the military works in this same manner. Here, officers did not have to address their supervisors as sergeant, lieutenant, etc. unless you were in trouble or in a formal meeting.

We were officers, much like officers in the Armed Forces. Dispatchers were somewhat subordinates to officers. At the sheriff's department, I actually got into trouble over failure to listen to a dispatcher!

I was on an Air Force base and following an Air Force security officer to their office and wanted to be polite. The dispatcher told me to return to the gate per a phone conversation and didn't realize I was at the scene, which is an entirely different matter. A sheriff's sergeant ordered me to return to the sheriff's office after the call, which was handled quite well by me. I thought after explaining the situation that all would be forgiven. With his prior Army experience, he showed me the duty manual, and it read that a deputy will obey the dispatcher regardless of the situation at the scene. I was noted as hardheaded for refusal to obey a dispatcher who, with a high school degree or GED, was now my supervisor! San Bernardino sheriff, I hope you have changed this duty manual requirement! A dispatcher could actually send a deputy to his death! "Paul 4, drive your patrol car off a cliff!"

"Paul4, copy?" "Paul 4, is your radio on?" "Copy my order?" Mere silence. "Sir, Paul 4 must have turned his radio off." It must be that stupid college degree he brags about.

San Jose police uses dispatchers to direct the officer, but the officer at the scene was the one calling the shots. Doesn't that make more sense? Have you ever known a civilian who was hired on a small police department, and the following week, they put on a uniform, and all of a sudden, they were a professional in criminal law and enforcement? If not, you need to listen to the dispatchers at the small city I reside in.

San Jose police also attend one week in CPT, continued police training, in a classroom or training facility each year. We look at the mistakes that San Francisco and other police departments make and then train for a better outcome. We train on felony car stops using actual paintball rounds loaded in 9mm shells. Believe me, when you're hit, you know it. I was actually hit on my ring finger and thought I broke my finger. These rounds hit you, and you immediately know it!

We do building entries, and there is a trainer that will shoot at you if you mess up, and you will feel the pain and will remember your sin. But police work is continuous training, learning, and making mistakes so one will not make them on the street and so the city does not have to pay millions in lawsuits over a bad shooting.

One other trait of San Jose police is a cap on special units. If one goes to the detective unit, you can only stay for three years. Then back to patrol for at least one year before you can apply for another special unit, such as motorcycles or vice or narcotics or homicide.

The officer has a wide scope of different experiences and is a well-rounded, experienced law enforcement professional. I believe Los Angeles has homicide detectives who stay at homicide for years. Or a traffic officer who stays in traffic for twenty-five years and his total expertise is writing traffic tickets? Not in San Jose. One needs to learn all aspects of law enforcement. A small department does not have the funds to always send officers to training classes.

Back east, you can watch some officers shooting at fleeing unarmed individuals. Inadequate training, uneducated, and underpaid. You get what you pay for! Maybe the dispatcher ordered the officer to shoot while sitting behind a desk and listening.

I want to add that the San Jose police dispatchers are the finest professionals in the world. They are intuitive, intelligent, patient, sensitive, and alert. They have to listen many times to sarcastic officers talking over the radio and talking down to them. I was made a temporary dispatcher for one month while at Victorville. I almost got into fights with deputies in the locker room and got a few citizen complaints. I would rather eat worms or work in the jail. Anything! It is a hard job, and I commend the professional demeanor of the dispatchers at San Jose police. They truly hire the best.

CHAPTER 19

———◇◈◇———

Patrol Assignment

Swing shift assigned, I made my way to the briefing room. At the time, the room filled up with about seventy officers. The officers sat down at the tables, facing the front of the room. Sergeants, lieutenants, and a captain stood along the wall. A sergeant gave briefing and called roll call. It was a pleasant time with jokes and jabs, mostly at other sergeants and maybe a lieutenant. The officers were placed in a good mood before going out into harm's way. I liked briefings and the joking.

A serviceman goes into battle for one to several years, seeing more harm than a police officer.

But a police officer goes into harm's way every day, and in my case, thirty-two years total. We see the worst in people every day. Even into retirement, one is still reliving events, and we become very cynical and bitter. Even by driving down the street, we can spot ugly things happening or about to happen. Our dreams from meeting with bad situations are relived with vivid memories. A lot of retirees are alone, single, and bitter. When driving down a freeway, one notices every single idiot driving a car. Many are meth users who can't go fast enough and begin cutting others drivers off and tailgating. It's not just dirty looking young males. It's mothers, fathers, business people, night clubbers, construction workers.

Anyway, armed and placed in a good mood from briefing, we return to the locker room to pick up our equipment and head to the garage for our assigned patrol cars. Once in the car, we check out lights, siren, and unreported damage by other officers. From here, we drive to central supply for a hand pack, a walkie-talkie, and a shotgun. Then we log on. "Control 6, Paul 1," and the dispatcher answers back, "6, Paul 1." We respond, "6, Paul 1. Badge number 2585, 10-8," meaning in service and ready for calls. Then we respond to our assigned area, which could be Eastside, central, or western divisions.

Then the calls come in which you hope day shift took care of before, so one can go hunting for crime.

Vehicle stops, pedestrian stops, anything you have probable cause to believe that a crime has occurred or about to occur. Looking and hunting and observing, going to locations that are known for high crime, etc.

Later that night, I got a call to meet with undercover narcotics officers in plain clothes in order to execute a search warrant. When the door is kicked, I'm the first one in with a uniform, so the crooks will know it's the police and not a rival gang or hoodlums. Narco officers usually have long hair and beards and dress in regular street clothes.

I met with the narco sergeant who said we would be doing a drug bust with Geraldo Rivera and news cameras. This was about 1987, and I didn't know who Geraldo Rivera was. The sergeant explained that he was the guy on 20-20 with the handlebar mustache. "Oh, yeah." Now I remembered.

Wow! I had made an arrest in front of Roy Rogers, and now I was going to do a bust with Geraldo Rivera! I love making arrests with famous people, and it would be on national television! Rivera was doing a show on drugs in the USA. I bet Rivera was just as excited to be working with a famous cop like me, as I was to be working with him—*not*. The show would be called *American Vice*.

Anyway, I was to go in first, and a cameraman was to follow right behind me. Remember, I said behind me, as in "me first, you follow." There were armed dopers inside, as in "dangerous." This meant that I might have to shoot someone. Nope, the cameraman still didn't get it. This was not a movie! This was the real thing. Nope, still went over his head.

I was to take the stairway up with the cameraman behind me and secure that area. The door was kicked and everyone yelled, "Police, search warrant." Somehow, the overexcited cameraman wound up in front of me and began going up the stairs. I thought *Cool, I have a human shield for protection.*

A Mexican national was lying on a bed with a .45 caliber pistol underneath the bed. I drew down on him, and he submitted to my arrest. This guy was high on PCP.

All arrestees, mothers, and children were brought down to the downstairs living room and sat down on the couch. Rivera was advised that it was now safe to come in for the televised interview. The children were crying, and Rivera showed the camera audience the stoned Mexican national's eyes from PCP influence.

From here, I went 10-8 from this call to handle any other calls pending.

A few months passed when I noticed that *American Vice* would be on primetime television. I made sure my TV had a blank VCR inserted in order to record the show. *Once Hollywood saw me in action, they would want me to be the new Clint Eastwood,* I thought. They cut most of my part out, only showing me handcuffing a poor PCP illegal felon for a few seconds. The camera did show my left side and good side though. I guess Geraldo must have felt threatened by me. Goodbye, Hollywood, and goodbye, red carpet.

*****

The Death of Two Police Officers

I was working day shift in the Paul district. This is located on the southern east side of San Jose. Close to noon hour and I was starting to think about code 7, lunch. All of a sudden, the dispatcher on the radio says, "Paul 6, Paul 7, Paul 4, Paul 2, you're assigned to respond to the downtown area near Santa Clara St. and 7th St." I answered back, "Paul 6 en route."

I arrived to see that Santa Clara St. was closed down to traffic. An army of patrol cars were parked on Santa Clara St., and there was crime scene tape covering sections of the street. I still didn't know what was happening. Downtown beat patrol was on a different radio channel, so I switched over to channel 5 on my hand pack. I could hear that homicide detectives were en route from police headquarters.

I began walking over to the crowd of police officers. I immediately noticed a man lying on his back.

Then I noticed that the man had on the same type of pants that I had on, with the white stripe going down the outer length of the pant leg. Then I saw what was once the officer's face. I was not prepared for what I had just seen. I have seen a lot of deceased people, but this was different. A part of me seemed to be lying on the asphalt parking lot.

I noted the location to be on Santa Clara St. at 5th St. This was a Winchell's Donut parking lot. The business has long been torn down, and the new present day city hall now stands at this location.

I met with a sergeant who said that the officer had made contact with a subject reported to be acting strangely. The person, a black male who was unarmed, got a hold of the officer's gun and killed the officer with his own gun.

When responding officers arrived, the suspect was now in the middle of Santa Clara St., and the suspect began shooting at officers with the deceased officer's gun. The responding officers returned fire and hit the suspect in the chest several times.

Another officer had arrived, but he didn't realize that that he positioned himself in the crossfire of responding officers. This officer was hit with friendly fire from the pellets of buckshot and hit in an artery of his body. That officer had been rushed to the hospital in an attempt to save his life. A radio broadcast for the public had been sent out for public blood donations. Many citizens arrived and began donating blood. Unfortunately, this officer passed away as a result of his wounds.

I was directed to start a door-to-door investigation of any witnesses on the south side of Santa Clara St. I wrote down names and addresses of all residents, whether they saw or heard anything or not.

I would later have to write on a police form and submit it to the homicide detail.

What happened that day left me feeling cold, shocked, and vulnerable. I vowed that whenever a potentially violent, unarmed man tried to wrestle my gun or made a maneuvere to overpower me while I was handcuffing that person, he would be shot! It would be him or me. If there was time, I would explain that to the suspect his choice. I have never had to go that far, but I did take time to educate the person, and I talked slowly in case the suspect was on a drug that would slow his decision-making. There is no such thing as an unarmed man when he is struggling with an armed police officer.

Single mothers, teach your children that they are to submit to police officers. It's actually a law!

We need this in a civilized society. Later, if the officer did wrong, one can sue the city or county, but your little angel or great, friendly neighbor will still be alive. And the bad officer will be brought to justice.

Officers, deputies, don't shoot at a suspect fleeing unless he is armed and the potential for human life would be endangered. Officers in California have been professional, but some of those overweight police officers back in other States seem really out of line. Remember, I said some. Most are professional.

The bottom line is: Come home, *alive*. You can face the attorneys and Monday night quarterbacks later. But you will be alive. Remember, "Blue Lives Matter!"

In memory of fallen officers, Gene Simpson and Gordon Silva, January 20, 1989.

*****

A Funny Thing Happened on the Way to Jail

Well, maybe not for the crook, but he put the smile and laughter out of the victim.

An illegal Mexican national felt it was a good night to commit a burglary. It was a cold December night.

I do mean cold! The suspect wanted to be Santa Claus, I'm sure of it. How does Santa gain entry?

Through the chimney. Pedro wanted to gain entry into a Mexican restaurant, and with all the Christmas movies going on television, what better way to enter and then help himself to the cash register. Imagine, all the hard work the owner and the employees had done, and all of it would soon be in Pedro's pocket! And he didn't even have to work for it. He would be able to buy Christmas gifts for his family and get himself a long-deserved gift as well.

Pedro carefully climbed to the roof of the building with a warm jacket to ward off the thirty degrees temperature. He removed the upper lid of the exhaust vent and carefully lowered himself down the tube. Pedro had to place his arms over his head to fit inside.

Oh, oh, about four feet down, Pedro found himself stuck. He managed to take his jacket off hoping that this would free himself from the imprisoning tube. Nope, Pedro couldn't move. He removed his shoes with hopes that he might climb back up using his bare feet to grip. Nope, he was stuck.

How would he explain his predicament? More importantly, how did he get out of this one?

Pedro would have all evening and part of the morning to think of a good excuse. The tube was so greasy from all the deep frying, as this was located directly over the oven. What would happen when the cook arrived the next day and turned on the oven? Would they be able to hear Pedro screaming? It seemed his goose was cooked, or rather, Pedro would be cooked.

Santa Claus had made it look so easy. But he did not possess the magic that St. Nick possessed.

The tubing tunnel began to get extremely cold, and he was in for a long night. Every time he moved, he would slip a little more. What a way to pass on into the afterlife. Was heaven as beautiful as they say? Would Pedro make it into heaven? Would he freeze to death?

The next day, the cook arrived and knew he would have to start heating the ovens in order to prepare lunch for the hungry customers, soon to arrive. Pedro had been confined for about eight hours.

"Help me!" It was oh so faint. The cook thought he was hearing things. "Help me," the voice said in Spanish. That's odd; there was that sound again coming from the vent over the stove. "Help me!"

Finally, the cook called up the vent, "Is someone up there?" "Yes," came the faint and exhausted voice.

"I'm stuck, please."

"But how did you get up there?" replied the cook.

"5 Mary 1," replied the dispatcher. I was on day shift in the Mary district. I answered, and the dispatcher went on, "Respond with fire to King and Story for a man trapped in the roof in a vent." "Copy, en route," I responded. Fire was short for the fire department.

I arrived and saw the ladder leading to the roof of a restaurant. I climbed up and met with firefighters on the roof. A smaller firefighter was lowered down the vent, and a larger fire fighter was holding him by his ankles. A second firefighter joined in and grabbed an ankle of the lowered firefighter.

Soon, they were pulling the firefighter upward, and he was clutching a scared Mexican national by the wrist. Pedro was free but didn't look well. Pedro was lowered onto the parking lot, and an ambulance awaited him.

I followed the ambulance to Valley Memorial Hospital and stayed with him as he was basically in custody at this point. Pedro was filthy with cooking grease, and they advised that he was suffering from exposure due to the previous evening. I stayed with him as he took a long hot shower in the hospital.

Once back to his bed, I made out my report and would be booking him for attempted burglary. Jail officers responded and would be watching him until he was cleared from the hospital. I had to deliver my booking paperwork to the main jail along with any personal property.

When Pedro's court date arrived, I showed up and learned that he was pleading innocent! His alibi had been that he was merely walking along when he was kidnapped by some bad hombres. They drove him to the restaurant and ordered him to climb to the roof and gain entry. He was to steal from the cash register and then give the money to them. If he refused, they would harm his family.

Somehow, a plea was reached, and I was not needed for testimony. I'm not sure if Pedro had to serve any more jail time. But I do know this, Pedro had already experienced justice.

*****

On another occasion, while still on day shift in the Mary district, I and other team members were assigned to assist fire with traffic control in regards to a house totally engulfed in flames.

Through investigation, it was learned that two people had been in the house and had burned to death as a result. It was later learned that the husband had been despondent over his marriage and wanted to commit suicide and take his wife with him. He obtained a five-gallon tank of gas and matches. When the wife was forced into the living room, he threw a match into the container. The gas container exploded and immediately engulfed the living room in flames. The wife never had a chance.

This was the Eastside of San Jose, and it could be a rough place.

Still another, this man had shot his wife then swallowed Drano. The crazy part was, I had watched the man being taken away in the ambulance, screaming. I would later learn that he had major burning in his throat, and his stomach had to be completely removed!

I saw many more suicides and cut as many as three down with the same pocket knife I had carried. There were indeed a lot of unhappy people out there.

One thing that is important is that a police officer sees all these horrors and still has to maintain his own sanity. He doesn't wait for Halloween to arrive; it's here all the time. An officer has to go home and then assume the role of husband and father. He or she must maintain patience, understanding, love, and sympathy while keeping his thoughts of the horrors back at work. Their spouse must also be patient and understanding and try to make the officer's time at home relaxing. Many times, this can't happen because of family problems and frustrations. I don't envy any spouse who marries an officer, and it takes a strong spouse to maintain a marriage.

My first marriage did not survive. I, however, maintained a close relation with my sons who are my friends to this day. I am now happily married and pushing towards our twenty-year mark as I write this book.

Patrol is one of the most dangerous and exciting part of police work. It is completely boring most of the time and can get terrifying and fatal in a few seconds. It can result in error where the officer only had a few seconds to respond, with Monday night quarterbacking being decided for several weeks.

Shift changes from days to graveyard can put further strain on the body and mind. People who serve a full thirty-year career are special.

Chapter 20

The Detective Bureau

My true interest in police work was to eventually promote into the detective bureau. Even though San Jose police does not recognize the bureau as a promotion, I felt it was one. One basically studies and takes a written test and then an oral test. The highest score will be the candidate they choose—kind of. If selected, the detective will serve three years then have to rotate back to patrol before one had test for another unit. Now, when I say "kind of," this means that friendships and personal bias has a lot to do with it. Rumors of a person being lazy or not a team player play into account. One cannot go to the unit and ask the sergeant or lieutenant if they don't have a chance, because they will always say that you do. This is because they want to appear unbiased and open-minded. Plus, they don't want the police union to come down on them and ruin their chances of later being promoted.

At most police departments, one can go to homicide and stay there for the remainder of their career such as Columbo. But with San Jose police, three years in homicide then back to patrol for one year, then one could reapply and test for homicide. San Jose police wants an officer with a well-rounded career with several different units.

San Jose police really made the patrol officer as the main element of law enforcement. He was not looked down as the bottom of the working force. Also, he was paid quite well, so the drive for promotion was lessened.

Patrol bids for shifts every six months. According to seniority, an officer bids for beat assignment, days off, and decides what shift he would like to work. With three days off a week, an officer could bid for a team with Saturday, Sunday, and Monday on day shift. This would take a lot on seniority for this. Also, one could decide what supervisor he would work for. Isn't that sweet? If they took away the possibility of being shot, it's not a bad job.

If one gets promoted to sergeant, they can expect to work grave-yard shift with Monday, Tuesday, and Wednesday off. So say good-bye to your family for a long, long time. For some, this is a bless-ing, depending on your marital status. But for the family man who believes in a strong union with spouse and children, this can be a burden. It depends on your priorities.

So the next time you ask a retired officer what rank he was, don't judge them by their rank.

Many of the retired brass retire with no marriage, troubled kids, and living in a one bedroom apartment. Their retirement checks get divided between several former spouses. It's a fine balance between family and career.

Also, there are many brass officers who could not handle the danger of patrol and were terrible officers and promoted to let the professionals handle the danger, while they judged from an air con-ditioned office.

Promotion is done by studying for a minimum of nine months, a lot of boring books not related to police work. Also, join a study group with a sergeant heading it. The sergeant will brag to the other lieutenants because you are now his or her personal student.

When you walk into the promotion oral board, you will already have a name, and judgment already began before your actual oral test. Learn to kiss butt. I never mastered this technique.

They should give a class in it. Also, learn good acting. If you hate a lieutenant, one could act like they like him and actually "look up" to the individual. This will bolster the lieutenant's ego, and in turn, they should like you. I guess that would fall under "advanced acting," and maybe they could start an academy award ceremony for best actors.

In all fairness, there are officers who I truly respect, and when they get promoted, they earned it.

I actually go fishing with a lieutenant who worked homicide and was an excellent investigator and interrogator. But he keeps forgetting that in our retirement years, I'm smarter and better at fishing and probably forgot more in life that he'll ever know.

While working a swing shift beat in the Sam district, I made my sergeant aware of the fact that I had an interest in the detective unit. I advised that I would attempt to do an extra good job investigating and follow up and show him results and excellent reports. Also, I knew that he was an alcoholic, so I made sure to attend all after work barbeques where beer was consumed.

Also, if he made a joke, I made sure I laughed extra loud. Red carpet, here I come!

I applied and attended a three-day course with the FBI giving the instruction. The class was a delightful class of serial killers, and the way they left a signature on all their killing crime scenes. We listened to actual victim's being tortured on recorded tape before being executed.

Many students went to hotel rooms that night while still being haunted by the screams of the innocent victims. We were taught in the area of victim abduction and slavery. I learned of suspect profiling. I learned that through profiling, one can tell sex, race, approximate age, and financial class of the suspect. The accuracy was in the ninety percent range!

Before I go on, let me explain that profiling race was done by area of the crime scene. For instance, if the area and abduction was primarily of a certain race, the suspect was usually of that race.

If the victim was learned to be stalked from a Hispanic bar and the neighborhood was Hispanic, there was a ninety percent chance of the suspect fitting in the bar and neighborhood.

A college student victim would usually be victimized by someone close to the college community who could fit in to the surrounding area. If a White House intern was taken advantage of, then I would start looking at members of the Democratic Party. Just kidding.

When we finally left the three-day classes, most of us were emotionally drained from the evil actions of sick individuals. I truly believe that their judgment day will come, and it will not be a pretty sight.

Armed with more knowledge, I began to apply for different units. I went to the burglary unit and met with the sergeant and lieutenant and announced my plans for possible assignment.

I applied for the juvenile unit also. There were no other units available at the time, so I left with a pamphlet of the workings of each unit. Also, I studied all penal code sections related to burglary and juvenile law concerns.

I took oral tests from each unit and waited for results. I was number three for burglary and number two for the juvenile unit. The problem with this is if there is only one opening in each unit, I would not be selected. The lists would remain active for six months and then expire, at which time you would have to reapply and retest.

*****

Missing Persons Unit

Within the juvenile unit is a different subunit of missing persons unit, which involved both missing adults as well juveniles. The female that was ahead of me was promoted to sergeant.

So she was dropped from the list, making me next in line. The sergeant started asking questions as to whether I was a team player and a suitable candidate for the opening. Both detectives were friends of mine who I worked with on prior patrol shifts, so I got a positive review. The call came to me, and now I was in! Detective Orok of missing persons. Probably my best unit and my best area of expertise. This would be one of the best units I had ever worked in my career.

I had to buy suits and ties and, of course, place them on my credit cards. During my time in patrol, I had worked at least ten hours of extra paid security jobs each week. This consisted of working in my uniform in schools and plazas. Maybe security at bars or night clubs. I kept my uniforms ready for these extra pay jobs, because there were just too many bills to pay at the end of the month. I had two small boys of one and three years of age and an unemployed and discontented wife, who liked using credit cards, not fully realizing that one had to make payments with high interest rates on these cards at the end of each month.

Another shocker was that I now had to work Monday through Friday and learned what a thing called commuter traffic was. Basically, one gets on a freeway expecting to drive at least sixty-five mph on a freeway, which was designed to do such. I believed that I had a right to do this, and I thought it was even written in the constitution somewhere. However, everyone else decided to drive on the freeway at the same time as me. What I found was that I was averaging twenty-five mph and had to drive sixty-five miles from Central Valley to San Jose. Where was the CHP, and why weren't they giving these idiots tickets for impeding my safe and speedy travel?

And people were involved in collisions! If these idiots didn't care for their own safety, at least they could wait for me to arrive at work before driving into other people! I tried screaming, waving my hands, and constantly changing lanes with the belief that a lane change would solve my problem. None of this was working, and I really wanted my way. If I was late for work by one hour, I wanted to civilly sue the driver for his or her stupidity for having me lose one or two hours of work. That would surly cure their bad driving habit.

My supervisor was also becoming impatient with me arriving late. I assured him that I had left two hours prior to work starting time. He came up with a brilliant idea. Instead of arriving at work at eight a.m., he suggested I arrive at seven a.m.! I could then leave work at four p.m.!

That extra hour did it! Sure, there were still idiots on the freeway, but there were far fewer. At least, this worked in 1989. One probably has to leave at two a.m. now. And does the governor want to fix this problem? No! He wants a train that leaves from Petticoat Junction to Los Angeles and arrives in twenty minutes! Once in LA, one will be held hostage in traffic for hours! Imagine a wino crossing the train tracks and a train is bearing down at two hundred mph plus! His drinking problem would be cured in a matter of seconds. What had this governor been smoking with Linda back in the day!

I also had the option of taking off Sunday and Monday for my weekend. This helped, and I was adjusting to the heavy traffic. My patience and maturity level grew from a one to a strong eight.

*****

The city of San Jose receives about five hundred missing persons per month at the time. At that time, we had three detectives and one sergeant to handle the case load. Most of the missing people were juveniles who were having troubles at home but would return after a fun weekend with friends. A few really did need help from an abusive environment with counseling needed or removal from the home.

I would estimate that one in every thousand reports turned out to homicide or suicide. So about every two months, I could be ready for the big one. I soon learned to tell the serious from the person willingly avoiding going home.

When judging the seriousness of a missing person report, I had to decide if someone was in trouble or if someone intentionally wanted to remain away from home. I didn't actually look for negative signs as much as I was looking for what people weren't saying or acting.

I learned that most people lied to police. Friends had been told what to say, mainly, "I didn't see nothing," and "I didn't hear nothing." So I would play along, sort of like what Columbo did on television.

If I called a boyfriend for the known whereabouts of a girlfriend, I would wait for the boyfriend to tell me that he was unsure. Or a best friend would offer the same lame excuse. Guess what? They just told me, in essence, that they knew fully where the person was and that they were not in danger. How? Because they forgot to act concerned about the disappearance. They would have called me five times a day asking me for an update. Or they would have called me or my police department incompetent.

You see, when OJ Simpson was accused of murder, he should have told news cameras how stupid the Los Angeles police were. Instead, he writes a book about why he couldn't have done it! Can you imagine if your wife goes missing and the police only want to accuse you? One would be in front of news cameras, calling their police a bunch of morons. City hall would get several calls a day from me. I would be quite angry! If I was innocent. If not, I would start making T-shirts to show what a caring, concerned husband I was.

The missing person report for Shiela Schermerhorn came across my desk in March. She had been missing since Thanksgiving Eve. Great. A three-month-old missing person's report. She had a history of leaving the home because of an abusive husband, and her children were getting tired of her absences. She was believed to have traveled to Las Vegas. That was it! There was nothing else for this detective to go on. But something stood out that grabbed my attention. The reporting party was not the husband or one of the kids. One of the kids actually attended a junior college. The reporting party were distant family members who were worried about their daughter, sister, brother, etc. Sheila would have no reason to avoid them.

The husband had actually worked at security at Evergreen College for a while, plus he was working for an attorney delivering subpoenas. The husband was a gunsmith or seller of guns and had a concealed weapons permit. This whole circumstance was different, and my gut feeling was in overdrive. I called the reporting party and asked her what her gut feeling was. I wanted to know how she felt about the disappearance. She feared the worst outcome. They were also in the process of hiring a private investigator.

It's at a time like this when you know God places sensitivity in investigators. They kind of sense something is wrong. You see, nothing escapes God; he sees all. Even if we had not found Sheila's killer, the killer will still have to deal with God almighty. If not now, very soon in the future. God can place a feeling in a sensitive believer which comes out as a certain gut feeling. Also, this report could have gone to two other detectives' desks. They were both out playing sports with PAL, which is our Police Activity League. They had no time for people who were missing, as far as I was concerned. Can you tell we didn't get along?

I walked into my lieutenant's office and told him about my concerns over the missing person.

He advised me to visit the captain of detective's office to give him an update. The captain told me to visit the lieutenant of homicide. The lieutenant did not seem to think anything was wrong because of the history with the woman leaving. If I had mentioned my gut feeling, he would not have believed me. If I had told him about feelings and God, he would have laughed.

In a time like this, it's better to tell everyone at the command level. When the stuff hits the fan, they will find it very hard to blame you when it goes down, because they were informed.

My sergeant was unaware of my progress in this matter. Not good for the sergeant who moved his friend into my desk when he was recently promoted and was trying to get me out of the unit.

The lieutenant knew I was the best missing person detective he had as I kept him out of hot water when the big cases came in. My immediate supervisor was missing and playing at PAL.

I had to borrow a detective from the juvenile unit to be my backup. I was going to meet Mr. Schermerhorn. My goal was to shock him into acting goofy—push him over the edge.

I already knew he would lie to me. I wasn't expecting the truth. Even the detective with me did not think he was guilty of any wrongdoing, but he was my friend, and I asked him to at least pretend that I might be right.

If you don't already know me from this book, I have a tendency to push people's button.

This would be naturally easy for me. Actually, it's God's fault. He made me like this, I think.

We left our coats in the car and had our guns holstered and our badges out. I wanted to intimidate the defendant. I was armed with a picture of Sheila, and I wanted to show it directly in front of his face when talking about her.

We approached the front door, and I knocked, but there was no answer. Mr. Schermerhorn was inside with his kids, but no one would answer the door. My detective friend wanted to leave, but I couldn't. I noted that the door may have not have been latched completely. I knocked harder and accidentally pushed, and the door accidentally opened. "Mr. Schermerhorn, are you okay? Mr. Schermerhorn? Oh, there you are! I was worried about your safety, because your door was ajar. I'm glad you're okay. Can we sit at your kitchen table so we can talk about your missing wife? And can you lie to me—I mean talk to me about the circumstances?" Actually, I didn't say *lie*, but I was thinking it.

The college-aged kid had seen me, and I asked him to talk with me. He seemed agitated and felt that his mother had merely abandoned the family. He went into his bedroom and slammed the door. I asked Mr. Schermerhorn to follow me into the police station so I could get a more detailed story of his wife. I needed to be on my own turf and not his. I did not have anything to hold him for suspicion, and Sheila could have very well walked in the front door at any time. Certainly, everyone at my department didn't believe me.

"Mr. Schermerhorn, I think something may have happened to your wife, and I want to investigate this immediately." I then showed him Sheila's photograph by putting it directly up to his face.

He agreed to go to the police station and needed to bring his ten-year old son with him as he had no babysitter. He wanted to drive his own car. I had no way to force him, but at least I was getting some cooperation.

I agreed to this. He knew he had his own rights and could not be forced.

Tom and I got into the unmarked unit and waited for Schermerhorn and his son to pull out into the street behind me. Tom stated that he did not feel Schermerhorn was a suspect in the disappearance of Sheila as he was getting into the car.

We drove several miles to police headquarters and were about half a mile away when Schermerhorn began driving straight instead of following me. At Mission Street and Guadalupe Ave., he headed north and away from us. I asked Tom, "What do you think now, Tom?"

"Where's he going?" I felt that he would head over to his attorney's office so he wouldn't have to be questioned by me.

I had no legal means to turn around in heavy Friday night traffic and effect a car stop.

I did not have a red light or siren in the car I was using.

I would later find out that he was carrying a pistol with his CCW permit, and there had been two extra guns in the car—all legal.

I drove to the police department and walked directly into the homicide office and informed the lieutenant as to what had just taken place. He advised that Schermerhorn was just acting goofy but that there were still no grounds to go after him.

I returned to the missing persons unit and found that everyone had gone home as it was after five p.m. I had a decision to make as far as telling my sergeant, who was now presently at home.

If he had walked into the office the next day without knowing the details, he would be in hot water.

Remember, this is the guy trying to get me out of his unit. Anyway, I decided I would call him at home and update him so the lieutenant would at least think he was doing some type of supervisor role. I never saw an enemy turn into my buddy as fast as this guy did. The sergeant on probation was now seeing why the lieutenant valued my service so highly and refused to transfer me.

I phoned the older Schermerhorn son at the home and asked if his father had returned with his ten-year-old son. He said no and felt it unusual for his dad to act this way. I asked him to ask his dad about his mom missing and what he knew. More importantly, I informed the son that I felt something bad may have happened to his mother and told him to cooperate with me so we could start getting some answers.

The following day, I was trying to get a plan together as to how approach this investigation.

The family relatives had hired a private investigator who was presently at the home of Schermerhorn. The family was cooperating fully with this investigator. Apparently, he had asked if there was anywhere in the house where Mr. Schermerhorn had insisted that no one went into. They told the investigator the garage area. When he opened the door, he could smell the immediate odor of a three-month-old decaying body.

The investigator called me at my office. "Hello, Detective Orok of missing persons." He replied, "Hey, I got your body here." I said, "What do you mean?" He replied, "She's wrapped in plastic under the car, in the garage." I said, "Get the family away from the garage area." He replied, "I already did, and we're all seated in the living room area." Apparently, this was an experienced, seasoned investigator who had found many bodies before.

My supervisor was in an interesting conversation with his buddy over PAL games, and even though I didn't want to interrupt a good conversation, I had to loudly explain that we had a body. I called dispatch and asked for a patrol unit to arrive at the scene to confirm. We turned on our handheld radios and turned to the channel involving the yellow district team.

The unit arrived and confirmed 10-55, indicating a confirmed dead body.

Homicide was en route, and missing persons unit was also en route. When meeting with the homicide lieutenant, he immediately looked at me and said, "You were right." Homicide would now be taking the case over, as it was now an apparent homicide.

While back at the office, a news reporter who I was familiar with, Betty, stopped by to talk with me so she could begin her story for the San Jose *Mercury News*. I have always trusted her and found her to be a great investigative reporter. Actually, she was better than some of the detectives who worked in the bureau.

I first had to tell her how I had no legal means to stop Schermerhorn on the night I questioned him. Only by making contact with him and pushing him over the edge would he finally do something stupid enough to direct suspicion on him. He had no obligation to comply with my requests. An attorney would advise him not to speak with me. I had to get him to start acting strange. I told Betty that if she made the report to make me look foolish, I will never have the open, friendly, informative conversations with her that we shared in the past.

The next day, I got a copy of the *Mercury News*, and she had done an excellent job in explaining the actions of the police detectives.

Next, my sergeant and "new buddy" and I were in several different offices being questioned by the captain, homicide, and again by the captain of detectives. I think the captain was trying to "burn" my lieutenant and that there was some kind of rift between the two. My lieutenant advised me not to go into the captain of detective's office without him present. The captain was trying to get me into his office without the lieutenant present. I could just feel the love between the two administrators. When the captain came directly to my desk to ask me to accompany him, he had known that the lieutenant was away. The lieutenant had already informed the secretary to call him on his cell phone if he was away. He would arrive several minutes later, hoping I hadn't spoken ill of the lieutenant. Actually, I told the captain of our large caseload of approximately five hundred cases per month and the lack of physical evidence in a missing person case. I explained that I worked off of gut feeling alone. I explained that I would keep the good lieutenant informed of such cases and that he always gave me whatever resources I needed to help me.

Later, my credibility rose to a nine whenever I walked into a captain's or a lieutenant's office, and I was given the authority to work the case with the other cases divided between other detectives.

It was learned later that Mr. Schermerhorn had left from following me to driving directly to San Francisco to spend the entire last weekend with his ten-year-old son. They played arcades and had a fun time. The ten year old was put on a train, alone, back to San Jose, where news cameras awaited. Mr. Schermerhorn was now missing. His car was found abandoned with two of the guns inside. I thought we would later find Mr. Schermerhorn dead from suicide and was relieved that the son was okay.

Some of the other units in the police department began to gossip over how they would have handled the case without knowing all the facts. Can you imagine a SWAT team knocking on Schermerhorn's door and placing him on the floor at gunpoint and Sheila walking in through the front door to question what they were doing? SWAT teams get sent to a call that they know there is an armed person and act accordingly. But what happens when you don't know and you have to play it by ear? You are investigating and it suddenly turns into a deadly situation?

You are then questioned by people making armchair decisions or officers gossiping without knowing the facts.

Several months later, Mr. Schermerhorn had still not been located. The popular show, *America's Most Wanted*, had picked up on the story. The television host, John Walsh, explained to the television audience that Schermerhorn was still outstanding and needing help. The media is a great resource for locating crooks and missing people.

A few days later, a park ranger from a popular park near Santa Cruz called in and said that there was a homeless man living under a bush that resembled the suspect. The suspect was forty pounds lighter and had a long beard. Officers from the crime scene unit went to the area and contacted the suspect. Sure enough, it was Schermerhorn.

Everyone in the different units wanted to take credit for the capture. Actually, it took a team and the news media to eventually bring the culprit into custody. This took a *Columbo*-type gut feeling, a family that finally cooperated, and a viewing television audience.

Many police officers and detectives not fully aware of the case like to gossip, and the more the story is told, the better it gets. Officers can be the worst of all gossipers. I've decided to include a story about three Baptist ministers who decided to go fishing on a small boat out on a lake.

The three ministers were fishing while the boat was anchored and the motor was off. It was a beautiful spring day, and it promised to give the anglers a lucky adventure.

Suddenly, one of the pastors suggested that they each share a secret that they could confide in each other. In return, they could pray for each other and hope for divine healing. The bond between the men was now formed. The first pastor explained that he had a drinking problem that he managed to hide from his congregation. The two other pastors assured they would pray for the pastor. The second pastor went on to explain that he was addicted to porn.

"Okay, Brother, we will keep you in our prayers." But the third pastor was not talking, and I will speculate he *may* have been a former police officer. Anyway, he pulled up the anchor and began to start the engine. The other two pastors wanted to know what his secret was. When the engine finally purred to life, the pastor explained, "I have an extreme problem with keeping secrets, and right now, I can't wait to get back into town!"

No, it's not my story. I actually heard this one in church. Don't overthink this. Some officers do too much gossiping without knowing the full detail.

*****

Whenever you take a family photo, please remember to take a proper pose.

The missing report got delivered to my desk. Apparently, two unlicensed men had decided to go fishing at Steven's Creek Reservoir. Neither knew how to swim. They did not bring life preservers.

They had an inflatable Marlboro raft, a case of beer, and two fishing rods. I'll mention again that they did not know how to swim. They were dropped off by a friend who had a car in the morning. Both men were already in their thirties. The friend had returned at five p.m. to pick them up as planned. Guess what? The fishermen did not return as planned. The friend waited for about one hour and decided to leave for the comforts of home. Can you already see the trouble brewing? One week later, the family was growing concerned. The fishermen still had not returned home, and a case of beer only lasts so long.

Worried, the family finally made out a missing person's report, which made it to my desk about one week later. I took the report into the lieutenant's office, because this was most likely a drowning situation. Once again, I was sent down to the captain of detective's office to give my heads up presentation. By now, it was apparent that my credibility had risen to being highly believable and credible based on my gut feeling. The captain was quite relieved to see that Steven's Creek Reservoir is in the county or sheriff's jurisdiction.

I merely had to send the report to the sheriff's department. They would investigate. I was told to go to the victim's apartment to try to obtain a picture of the victim. I arrived and met with the mother of the missing person. The only picture she could find was one from the holiday season. The missing person had been seated on the couch holding a baby. The man's arm was raised, and he was extending his middle finger to the viewing audience—flipping the bird.

The baby looked so cute sitting in his lap. With this picture, I had been instructed to go to the *Mercury News* and the local television station so it could be viewed by the public.

Perhaps someone had seen them; maybe given them a ride home. When the picture showed up on the local news, they had apparently cut off the extended arm of the victim. The victim looked like any ordinary loving uncle holding his beloved nephew with one arm.

Then the rumors began. Some detectives felt that the two men had staged the disappearance to avoid something. I ran computer checks to make sure they did not have any pending jail or court appearances. Neither were married, so they did not have to avoid any marital obligations.

I believed that both men could be found with the help of a scuba team.

The first body floated to the surface in five weeks. A few weeks later, the second body floated to the surface. Every time I see a Marlboro raft tied to the roof of an SUV, I always will remember the two men without life preservers.

*****

The Wilson Brothers

Honor your mother and father so that you may enjoy a long life.

The report came across my desk about one week after their disappearance. It was not ordinary.

The reporting party was not a family member but a coworker. I could mentally see bells and whistles going off in my head. Dad and Mom were both missing! The two adult sons living at home were not the "worried" reporting party. Hopefully, you're starting to think like a detective.

I phoned the reporting party, who was a female who worked with the wife. She explained that Mrs. Wilson (not her real name) was with an abusive and alcoholic husband. Mrs. Wilson actually worked two different jobs in order to stay away from the husband and keep the peace. Mrs. Wilson never missed work. If she did, something was wrong!

Back into the lieutenant's office I went. I needed to make contact with the sons, and I needed a detective as a backup. Al Rivers was my partner, and he did one year with the San Diego Chargers in 1974. I could use a former football player in case things went bad.

We made contact with both sons at their home in the foothills of East San Jose. I asked if I could come in and talk with them. Prior to making contact with the sons, I had alerted Sgt. Dennis Lucco, who was the liaison with the news media. He felt that I was speculating over finding them both deceased. Sgt. Lucco had his sights on a lieutenant's promotion.

Seated at the kitchen table, I questioned both adult sons, who said that Dad and Mom had left in the family minivan and had not returned. They did not seem concerned.

I felt that we would eventually find the van with victims of a murder/suicide inside.

I finished my interview and made sure that the van and the license were in the nationwide computer system associated with a missing person/suspicious circumstance situation.

That same afternoon, a few blocks away, a jogger had been jogging and noticed a van with a substance resembling blood dripping onto the street. All of the surrounding streets had a large amount of cars parked on the streets. A minivan blended right in with no one being suspicious, except for the odor and leakage.

Patrol went to the scene and found both people inside. They had been shot. Homicide was now en route. A homicide sergeant asked me to drive both sons to the police department for routine questioning. I had developed a rapport with both sons, and they would feel more comfortable with a known face.

I stayed with both young men until three a.m. out in the hallway of the homicide unit. They had gone right through without dinner, and I felt that we could at least go to the second floor where our police cafeteria had vending machines. I returned and both homicide detectives wanted to know why we had left. I explained that both men had learned that their parents were dead and they had gone without dinner. It was the least that I could do. They were not suspects—or so I thought.

That's when the sergeant finally decided to tell me what was going on. Apparently, the crime scene unit had come to the house to process it in order to be thorough in the investigation.

In the filthy house, they found that the kitchen had been thoroughly cleaned. They processed the kitchen using a process with ultrared lights and were able to see remnants of blood splatter. Both parents had been shot in the kitchen. The bodies were carried out to the van.

Both sons' shoes had been washed in the washer. However, the blood still appeared on both shoes.

Nice of homicide to give me this information. Both sons were suspects. They allowed both sons to return home without telling them that they were under suspicion. Normally, the detective calls the district attorney who advises the sons to be released so the crime scene and evidence can be processed properly without the clock ticking and done in a more thorough manner.

Warrants are them issued at a later date. There is no flight risk in this case and no risk of further harm.

In the next several days, I received several calls with witnesses saying that the sons were having a party at the house. There was also a large life insurance settlement coming, so they did not have to worry about employment. Life was good—or so it seemed. A few months later, the arrest warrants came in, and both sons were arrested.

*****

Backgrounds

As a detective, I had the extreme pleasure of working in the background unit. Here, a detective researches candidate's background for possible employment for a recruit police officer.

It was absolutely interesting. Here is something that one can't study for. You are either a candidate or you're not. You don't exactly fail. You're just a nonselect.

I came on a temporary, three-month assignment to help regular backgrounders with an overloaded caseload. I was given about twelve candidates and had twelve weeks to have them ready for possible hiring. My training detective was a pleasant and funny woman named Sharon. She advised to get all of the referral letters mailed out within the next few days. Letters need time to get delivered, answered, and mailed back to go into the hiring folder. This could take several weeks with the twelve-week timeline. I thought that this was a waste of time, because the candidate would be listing favorable friends who would only say positive things about the candidate. But it would get better. Later, I could get out into the field to knock on doors and visit neighbors, ex-girlfriends, ex-spouses, ex-employers. With employers, the smaller employer, the better. How would the candidate treat customers when they worked at McDonald's? Or how about the small hobbies shop?

If the candidate was testing for another department, what was said to that background detective? If a person wants to be a good liar, they will have to have a good memory.

I focused a lot on whether the candidate was an arrogant bully. Did they steal?

Did they use drugs? Heavy drinker? What about driving history? Driving maturity?

Also, credit history? Did they live within their means, or did they need things that they could not afford?

I hear a lot of candidates who did not get over the background and tell friends and family members that they answered a question wrong, so they failed. This is incorrect.

One doesn't fail a background. They are just passed over for more suitable candidates.

San Jose police pays over a six-digit yearly salary. They can afford to hire the best suitable.

Even after a person is hired, one hopes that the candidate will not let the badge get to their head or turn into army drill sergeants. I'm sure we all have met officers like these. This is the wrong place to become a bully or to develop apathy for crime victims.

This is the wrong place to act like a marine drill sergeant, because you were not tough enough to handle a lifelong career in the Marines, and now the public has to pay for your weakness.

I will share a few candidates I investigated, and everyone surprised me. Some looked squeaky clean when I opened their folders. Later, I found they were liars, thieves, bullies, dopers, and other miscellaneous mental problems. Others, I thought, would wash out in a day, and they turned out to be outstanding citizens and excellent police officers. You just don't know with a person until you visit with people who know them. My job was to weed these people out so they didn't do damage to the police department or hurt citizens.

One candidate was an Army private with a beautiful letter from his supervisor explaining what a great soldier he was, who passed all federal background investigations and security measures. Be careful when a federal employee says someone or something is secure.

Anyway, I found that he had worked a small hobby store in the Fresno area. There had been money missing from the register on several occasions. The owner thought his son had taken the money. The owner received a phone call from a background investigator from San Francisco police saying that the candidate admitted to taking the money but explained that he returned the money to the owner. The owner told me he never received any money or admission of guilt. This candidate was also a terrible liar, because he forgot to let me know what he had told San Francisco police. One has to have a good memory to be a good liar. Nonselect. This candidate would have to remain in the army. He would never become a police officer. At least his supervisor liked him. He also had a toy model worth a few hundred dollars that he had stolen from the store. I asked my supervisor if I could attempt to get a warrant for possession of stolen property against him, but I was told to let it go and to begin investigating the next candidate.

*****

The next candidate was a pretty female who chose to wear a short dress and high heels. This was an initial interview and not a date. Prior to coming in, one is mailed a large envelope with numerous forms. Lots of information is asked about prior jobs, spouses, boyfriends, neighbors, criminal history, driving record, etc. Also, a signed document for permission to check the requested information. All other police departments that the candidate is applying for and status of the hiring board. If the candidate is being background checked by another department, then the name and phone number of the police background investigator too.

The princess sat down and crossed her legs and gave me a driver's license. That was it! No other paperwork. Are you kidding me? You can't be serious! You want a job as a police officer!

This is a very serious occupation. This isn't an interview for a bartender or hair stylist. I thanked her for coming in and suggested she could leave, and I would call her for further.

She had filled out some paperwork at a prior meeting with a classroom introduction class. I asked about a prior vehicle crash she had been involved in. She advised that she had been driving on a mountain road, and a squirrel ran onto the highway. She tried to avoid the rodent and overturned the car. This had been done at three a.m., and I don't believe squirrels run around at night due to the danger of being prey.

She had put in an application for San Francisco police and was being background checked there. I phoned the background investigator, and we compared notes. Remember I said that to be a good liar, one has to have a good memory? The princess had told San Francisco police that she had been drinking in Tijuana and someone slipped something into her drink. She became unconscious, and friends placed her in a car and ran for the border. Border officials from the US saw her condition and called for an ambulance. This poor candidate had nothing but bad luck I guess. First, a squirrel, and now, this. She failed to tell me about this adventure, and she had failed to tell San Francisco about saving the squirrel's life and ruining the paint job on her car. She would never succeed in becoming a police officer.

I was going to suggest that she put in an application for one of *Charlie's Angels* but then thought better of it. *Charlie's Angels* had all been police officers, and she would never make it to that level.

My next candidate had been a straight up candidate—or so it seemed. We investigate a person's financial maturity. He had a family with kids and a job which he was able to point out every violation and mistake of the owner. However, he would never admit to his own mistakes or discrepancies, as the employer had advised me. He was heavy in debt so he decided to declare bankruptcy. So he basically erased all his mistakes then went on with life. Somehow, he managed to gain several thousand dollars to pay his way through the police academy and apparently felt he was a shoe in for any police department. I had a problem with his arrogance and failure to be lenient with others but always seemed to know how to minimize or forgive his own transgressions.

Finally, at the lie detector interview, I watched as he faced the lie detector technician who happened to be an older Asian woman. He was not aware that I was watching him and was asking the questions through the technician. He looked at her in an arrogant, questioning manner. I mean, who was she to question this remarkable young man? When responding to the hiring board, I mentioned his arrogance and explained his unsuitability for employment. We actually had a lieutenant with the department, who I will introduce in a later chapter, who loved to make life miserable for others but could never see his own faults. Anyway, this candidate with his post academy education did not make the San Jose police. A part of me felt that he might make it as a private investigator or Army security guard.

Maybe a private investigator would not suit this individual. Remember the arrogant lieutenant I just described? He retired and tried his hand at investigating a case. He actually investigated a case without using proper discretion. The newspaper reported that his wife, who had been a district attorney prosecuting the other side of the crime, now had her husband investigating the other half of the situation, creating an extreme conflict of interest. The newspaper reported that her lieutenant-husband would no longer be investigating in the county of Santa Clara.

I was appalled at the indiscretion of the retired lieutenant and hoped that by eliminating the last candidate, I would prevent another embarrassment to the San Jose police department.

This was very unusual. A candidate came across my desk—a young black man, who worked as a nonsworn officer for Oakland police department. Why wasn't he a sworn officer? Both parents had been in trouble. Who had raised him? This was a slam dunk. I would go into Oakland in one morning on a Saturday and look at his file with the police department.

From there, I could check with neighbors and find out he was a partier, maybe into meth or cocaine!

Boy, was I wrong! Always let the investigation lead you to the truth. You may go into an investigation with preconceived thoughts, but chase the truth and you will find it. I drove to Oakland police department and identified myself. They gave me a room to sit, and they presented their employment records and evaluation before me. This poor guy was getting written up for walking outside without his hat on and other very petty things. Nothing positive. Yet he was noted for always being polite to citizens. He attempted to get hired as a regular sworn officer, but there was always something petty written up about him.

I went to interview neighbors at his apartment, and they had only good things to say about him: very polite, modest, patient, kind. Wow, but how did he turn into this fine, stable individual? How could someone grow up in Oakland and not use drugs? The media always had me believing that drug users were victims of their environment. As President Trump would say, "Fake news."

I found out that he was raised by an aunt who had him attending church on Sundays.

She must have taught him about being respectful and working hard, avoiding drugs and gangs. Think about it! This woman would have had to play the role of father and mother and provide him with self-esteem in a bad environment. What a great woman!

Every time I called him on the phone and requested additional documents, those documents were in the mail that day with a phone call and him advising me that they were en route.

What a great attitude! When I looked at his grades, he was somewhat below average.

Before the hiring board, they were concerned that he would not make the academy. I explained that his cooperation and courtesy were excellent and felt that he would not be at the head of the class but that he wanted the job bad enough to get passing grades. I thanked the board and walked out of the room. My job with backgrounds was finished, and I would be returning to missing persons as this was only a temporary assignment. I phoned the candidate at his home and explained that they might not hire him over the grades, but I explained that if he did get hired, he would have to work harder than ever and that he owed this to me. I knew he would not let me down.

A year or two later, when I returned to patrol, he was working his own patrol beat and doing great. Later, he went on to working in the gang unit and was a top producer. Last I saw him, he became sergeant. If he's not a lieutenant, it's because he never tested. I wanted to thank Oakland police for writing negative things about him so that we could hire him and have an outstanding police officer. Please, send us more!

Another very important thing about this individual, he never forgot about the fact that I went to bat for him, even years later. The most important thing about a man or woman is to have a good attitude and be thankful for everything you have in life. It will show for others, and they will want to hire you. Have an arrogant attitude and you'll notice you won't have a lot of friends or coworkers or even a job!

*****

Back to Missing Persons and Juvenile
Crimes and General Crimes

I was placed in juvenile crimes for a very short term. I hated juvenile crimes. Kids always commit crimes with several other juveniles. When I interrogate them and gain a confession, I write it down in the police report. Later, they get together with the other kids and devise a story that sounds more like they are innocent of the crime being investigated. They then tell their parents that the detective was lying about their confessions while being interviewed.

The parents then believe their "darling" kids, and so I can now be assumed of being a liar from several youths with each having a set of parents as well.

When interviewing a juvenile, I first give a speech about being honest and speaking only the truth. Then I gain my confession. The parents don't want to believe their kids are bad; the kid's friends think they were stupid for telling the truth. The family attorney thinks that the kid was stupid for telling the truth. So I'm the bad guy. The parents and family attorney feel much better with me being the bad guy. The kid avoids punishment. I can almost hear Hillary saying, "What's wrong with that?"

Here is what's wrong with that, Hillary. Usually, the crime is not that serious. Maybe vandalism or minor battery or theft. By admitting to a minor crime, the juvenile will learn the value of doing what is right and later becoming an honest adult in later years. In contrast, by lying, a juvenile will most likely become a crooked adult who matures into a bigger liar with more serious crimes.

For instance, let's say a middle-aged wife is aware of her husband cheating with interns working at, let's say, the White House. She approaches the young woman and accuses the young woman of being a liar and fabricator of the truth, even though the middle-aged woman knows that her husband is a womanizer and has been for a long time. You see, this middle-aged woman did not become a liar when she needed to protect her roaming husband. She became a liar at a very young age when she learned that lying had helped her in numerous occasions and may have even prompted her to become an attorney. Okay, that was insensitive for attorneys, and I apologize for comparing your occupation with the Clinton's. But can you see how admitting I was wrong about attorneys and then apologizing for my transgression made me a better person? Also, when a juvenile avoids one punishment, the payback may be ten times worse.

*****

Paybacks

I received the report at my desk in the juvenile unit. I was assigned to investigate juvenile crimes in Almaden Valley, an upper middle-class section of San Jose consisting of many millionaires and people of great wealth. There are many great people who live in this area, but there are also some very arrogant individuals who let their wealth get to their heads.

A husband/father went to get the newspaper from the driveway in the early morning hours.

He noticed something very unusual. His daughter's Honda Civic was resting on its side. He couldn't remember teaching her to park the car in this manner. He preferred to have the car resting on all four wheels. He questioned his daughter and learned that she had not left the car parked in this manner. A felony vandalism report was made and sent to me.

I began by questioning the daughter. She admitted to being social at the high school with a certain football player. She admitted to occasionally waving at him with her middle finger.

The football player would then yell out something derogatory. Now, her car was totaled by being flipped on its side. She gave me names of the boy and his friends on the high school football team. Upon planning to interrogate the football players, I had to consider the fact that these guys would be team players. They would also have high self-esteem. Also, one of the suspects' fathers was a deputy district attorney. They would be able to ask his daddy how to talk to the bad detective.

I planned to interrogate the players at the high school but knew that the principal loved his players as they had the school leading in football. I knew I had no chance at solving this crime but decided to take my best chance. My supervisor was informed, and I expressed my concerns. He advised me to call the dean of students, who he knew, and the dean was raised on the east side of San Jose and cared more about truth than the prestige of the football team. I asked my supervisor to accompany me and to have the dean present during the investigation. I knew I would be getting a complaint for my investigation so my supervisor would not have to question me later, because he would be with me.

Anyway, the interview went as planned. They either lawyered up or said that they didn't know a thing about the incident. Just like a carefully planned play on the football field.

The girl must have received all kinds of sarcastic gestures from the team in the following days. I had yet to talk with the key player who had planned the event. This boy's parents had great wealth and live on the hillside with a helicopter pad!

The mother agreed to meet with me in the office of the police department. At the time, the juvenile unit was in disarray with cabinets and scattered paperwork lying around. To get to my desk, one had to walk around a maze of filing cabinets and desks. It once had taken me ten minutes to find my way to the bathroom. I had marked my path with a Magic Marker so I could find my way back to my desk in record time.

The mother appeared, dressed elegantly with a mink and Louis Vuitton purse in hand. Her angel was with her. I made sure she sat on an office chair with a tilting backrest and gave the better seat to the hero football player. I advised him of his rights. She spoke for the gallant football hero. My son will not speak with you, and you will have to talk to my attorney. She got up, and I sat in amusement, watching her try to walk out in an arrogant gait with her hero in tow.

She cleared the first filing cabinets but became confused in her arrogant exit. She would soon need my assistance, but I would first make sure she humbled herself to ask. She walked back to my desk and asked for help. I showed her to the police exit. My case was shot, and I had expected such. But to watch her fumble for the exit made it almost worth it. Guess what?

It got even better! Remember I said it is better to correct a youth's action than let it grow into something worst?

About a month later, my phone rang, and I was speaking with the father of the suspect of the overturned car. Remember the mom with the mink coat? Dad was highly upset as his son was now a victim. The son was presently in surgery, getting his broken jaw repaired and would be in a lot of pain, not to mention a wired-up jaw for several weeks. I asked what had happened.

The dad explained that the victim of the damaged car had a childhood friend who had a problem with extreme violence. This friend had grown up in juvenile detention centers most of his life. Apparently, the friend wanted to meet the football hero. An argument started, and the friend then took a golf club out of the trunk of the car and proceeded to dislocate the hero's face. Police had already arrested the friend so there was nothing else left to be done.

I was hoping that the friend also chose his Fifth Amendment rights when police questioned him.

I told the dad that I was extremely sorry for his son's injury. I told him that as a father, he should have encouraged his son to tell police the truth and pay for damages. I explained that they need a father, not an attorney. I explained that it never would have gotten to this level if his son had confessed to his wrongdoing. I told him that his wife had appeared with his son and had been quite arrogant. He explained that they were in the process of getting a divorce.

The lesson to be learned here is that sometimes, having a team of attorneys and money will not always help you. Because sometimes, street justice will take over. The dad lost, the arrogant mother lost, and the principal lost. The team lost. The suspect? He scored a touchdown and went back to an environment that he was familiar with. He didn't have to be worried about a lawsuit, because he never owned anything. The victim of the damaged car? She probably got a new car! The football player arriving back at school couldn't say anything about the girl, because his mouth was now wired shut and guaranteed to insure at least several weeks of verbal argument silence on campus. Case closed.

Like I said, I hated juvenile and went back to missing persons. Prior to leaving the detective bureau, a personal problem came to me, which broadsided me. I wasn't expecting it.

CHAPTER 21

———◇◈◇———

Life Happens

I was seated at my desk, and the phone rang. It was my now ex-wife. "Don't come home, I've changed the locks and have a restraining order against you." Actually, the marriage had never been happy after the honeymoon stage. We had two boys, who were five years and eight years at the time. We had gone to counseling several times. We had gone to outpatient drug counseling, and mama wanted her wings and freedom back. When I left the house, I was not involved in any knockdown argument nor did I threaten violence. We discussed separation, but I was going to stick to my vows of marriage commitment. I was now a homeless man. I never had an affair, so this really knocked the wind out of me. I would have to find a bridge in which to live under where I would be welcome.

The reason this chapter is so important is because this is a story of survival. This may save your life or your spouse's life! I'm not talking to just police officers but all humanity. Life happens; get ready for it—survive.

In thirty-two years of law enforcement, I've known more officers who have killed themselves, and sometimes their spouses as well, than at the hands of criminals. We are trained to protect ourselves from criminals, but we are never given training in how to protect us from us.

I have seen officers get the notice to vacate then go ballistic. One officer drove home in a patrol unit and went upstairs and began throwing items out of the window. Because it was out of San Jose, the city police had to respond to stop him. Another officer shot his wife and placed her in the trunk of a car and drove the car several blocks and parked the car. The car was found in the sheriff's district, so they began the investigation. The officer who I had worked with on patrol a few times later turned the gun on himself.

A woman and fellow officer had an argument with her husband and turned her gun on herself. She was on the same patrol team as me, and I found her to be an excellent officer.

She defused many family disturbances but failed to protect herself from herself. Life happens, and there will be a dark shadow over you for a long time. Hang in there, and the sun will shine again. Even if you don't think it will, it will still shine again. Don't trust your feelings at the moment. Just get through each day. Get professional help if you need to get through the grief. Living under a bridge is not all that bad, and the wine can be quite tasty while sharing it with newly met friends.

My greatest worry was actually not for me, but for my sons. Who wants to grow up in a split family? I didn't care about myself; I cared about them growing up with psychological problems. At thirty-eight years of age, some men are worried about going through a change of life where they need a snazzy car and a younger wife, maybe a condo at the beach and some hair plugs. Life is drifting away, and they want to start out new, to find whatever will make them happy. Maybe have old college buddies come over with women.

Me, I wanted full visitation rights. I wanted to see my sons grow up. If I wasn't working, I wanted to be with them. I wanted to take them and watch their baseball games. I wanted to supervise their homework and make sure they had their grades up.

Anyway, after the famous phone call on November 13, 1993, I decided to plan things out from there. I phoned her and said I would stay at a security office, which had a bunk bed, until I had a day off. Then I would drive home and obtain the truck/camper and live in it in the police parking lot. I would then shower in the police gym until December 1, 1993. A two-bedroom apartment would then be open for me. I then purchased a bunk bed for the boys and a small television which were both used. My apartment was filled with second-hand furniture. For my car, I purchased a 1994 Geo Metro! These are so small that a 1960s VW Bug looks big while parked next to it.

My social life was over. No one would ever want to go out with thirty-eight-year-old divorced man with two sons and a Geo Metro. When I was eighteen years old, I drove a 1971 Mach 1 Mustang. It had a Cleveland 351 cubic inch engine. Twenty years later, I'm in a Geo Metro with a three-cylinder engine. I could drive on the freeway at eighty mph, and the CHP were too embarrassed to pull me over.

The reason I'm telling you this is because things get bad in life. The next time you're feeling like quitting, think about me in a Geo Metro flying by at seventy-five mph. Hang in there and don't give up. Don't harm yourself and don't harm your ex-spouse. Yes, I know you own a gun and also a shovel, but don't listen to those voices. Yes, I know Nevada has a lot of barren real estate but repeat these words: "Get behind me, Satan."

You see, we are all capable of extreme violence. But we choose to listen to the better choice of reason. It's even easier when you believe in a supreme being. Yes, I'm talking about God. There is a future hope, even when we don't immediately see it. And as for the ex-spouse? God will take care of that. God hates divorce.

"But I don't believe in God!" Okay, let's look at what you believe occurred in the universe and mankind. I was actually taught this in school!

*****

Atheism

The belief that there was nothing, and nothing happened to nothing, and nothing magically exploded for no reason, and then a bunch of everything magically rearranged itself for no reason whatso-ever into self-replicating bits which then turned into dinosaurs.

This makes perfect sense, right? Wow, I'm ready to start using drugs. Maybe buy some violent videos and act out my anger on innocent people.

Or maybe you go a little farther and say, "Well, I believe in God and the Ten Commandments." Great, but so does Satan. Wow, you two could be buddies, maybe go out for a drink! Satan talked to Jesus all the time, even tempted him! Please read this sad story about Satan talking with a housewife.

The housewife had a problem with shopping and overspending on items that she didn't need.

The wise husband, knowing God's Word, counseled his wife by telling her that Satan was telling her that she deserved the item and could overspend. Satan knew this would cause strife in the union between man and wife. The husband said, "When you hear the voice, tell it, 'Get behind me Satan!'" The voice would then leave her mind. Sure enough, at the mall, the wife spotted an overpriced dress that they could not afford. She put it on and looked fabulous in it. The voice came, "Buy it, you deserve it." The wife was ready. "Get behind me Satan!" That evening, the husband discovered the dress in the closet. The husband was shocked and questioned his wife. The husband demanded to know if his wife had spoken the command for Satan to get behind her. "Yes, I told Satan to get behind me." The husband demanded, "So what happened?"

The wife spoke, "When I told him to get behind me, he did." "Great," declared the husband, "so why did it not work?" The wife explained, "When he got behind me, he said that it looked even better from the back!"

You see, you have to know God's Word and plan for you. And when you hear Satan's, you will know not only that it's him, but you will be able to tell him where he can go. He's going to wind up there anyway, eventually.

Did you know that in AA meetings, they actually tell the members that they need to believe in a higher source other than themselves in order to beat their addiction? Let's look at half-truths. You're told these when liars don't want to go as far as lying. Ever see a bumper sticker that said "Life sucks and then you die"? This is a half-truth. You see, life can be extremely hard. But if you go on, afterlife gets extremely pleasant. That's the second part of truth. For some, it will get even worse. Many people have died for several minutes and came back to life, only to report that they did not wish to come back to life after seeing paradise. Others were so scared of their future destination that they made an extreme change in their behavior and beliefs.

One older woman with extreme body pains finally died and was pain free. She was pain free and got to meet with her beloved husband. Her church came to her hospital bed and began praying for her. Against her will, she was made to come back to her painful old body and was back in her hospital bed. She was mad at the congregation for weeks. She informed everyone that they were not to pray for her again. The next time she died, she was now able to enter a much better nonpainful environment.

How does faith help us as we're living? Well, I believe God allowed me to become a police officer.

I believe that he sees all and me included. I have waited numerous hours with dead bodies while waiting for the coroner. I have never stolen jewelry or money from the deceased. Yet we have officers that have done so. I have never stolen dope from the evidence locker nor have I shot and killed unarmed men who were running from me. Yet there are officers that have done so.

I have never had affairs with women because of my authority nor taken advantage of female police explorers. Yet—well you get the picture.

You see, faith is what keeps us honest. It's what keeps us moving on in a bad marriage when you know you can do better. It's what keeps us spending time with kids instead of wanting to please ourselves with the younger, sexy secretary who we could run away with. It's what makes us love our families more than we love ourselves. There is a spiritual world working against us and for us at the same time. One half wants you and your family destroyed. The other half wants to help you and give you joy. It sometimes makes you wait. It loves you and your family.

It has to be so hard to be spiritually dense or a nonbeliever. I mean, things are happening all around you, and you can't see it. It's like a small child who is playing in the front yard with a ball and you have already told them not to run out in the street if the ball goes there. The child is not aware of the fact that there are cars that won't be able to see them and could kill them.

"But Daddy I don't believe in cars! They can stop in time, and I'm not going to believe because, I can't see that happen to me."

"The Bible is all fairy-tales. Christians are all bigots. They're weird." Actually, I've gained more wisdom by reading through the Bible. I actually feel quite foolish to have waited almost forty years to have done so. The officers who have been arrested or have hurt their families for their own selfish reasons, these people do not believe in a spiritual world. But keep in mind that the spiritual world is still alive and active all the time, even if you don't believe it!

When the ball goes out into the street, don't run after it. Even if you don't believe it's dangerous.

When is the most dangerous, evil time of the year? It's not Halloween, and it's not New Year, and it's not spring break. It's Christmas! Ask any police officer. Why is that?

Family disturbances are at all-time high, because families are getting together. They may not actually like each other, but they're caught up in the holiday frenzy. Suicides are at an all-time high. People watch the Hallmark channel and see delightful couples falling in love and living happily ever after.

Families are visiting from out of state, and delightful spirit is in the air. But what about the people who don't have families? Or if they do have families, are they dysfunctional? What about people with drinking and temper problems?

Suicides go way up and I mean *way up*. But something else is going on. Something evil is occurring, and our so-called friend who answers on the first ring seems to have enormous power at this time of year. You see, we're celebrating a glorious event. The birthday of the Savior is being celebrated! That may be good for you or man-kind, but imagine if this Savior is the one who will eventually send this spirit into hell! And that spirit happens to be the devil. Wouldn't you be angry and active in the world? You would want the people to focus on Santa Claus and let them know that they deserve happiness. If they don't have money, then they deserve to shoplift, steal, break into cars, kill, argue.

Remember the grown man and his nephew who I invited into jail on Christmas day? His brother was not worried about his son or brother being a thief. He was more worried that they be released so they could come home and open their well-deserved presents! Can you understand why I wasn't that big of a fan on Christmas day? What a relief after January arrived.

Anyway, Christmas is about celebrating the birth of Jesus. This is a Christian holiday that anyone can celebrate. We have distorted this beautiful holiday into something that is about greed, envy, impatience, demanding that we be made happy or else, mainly selfishness.

And for police, it's a dangerous time of the year. If you have any spiritual clarity, can you see the battle that's going on in the spiritual realm? But Satan does not want you to think about that. He wants you to think about Santa Claus and good children getting toys.

You know what gives me joy during the holiday? My wife and I buy a goat and two chickens for a family in Africa! I got a responding letter back telling me that two families would be sharing these animals. Can you imagine that? It stops one from feeling bad during the holidays. All these people want is eggs and milk in the morning. Now that is the true Christmas spirit.

In closing this chapter, I want to encourage and challenge you to read the Bible in one year. I want to have you start talking to Jesus through prayers in everyday life. Share anything, a worry, a hope, a blessing, a need at any time, while you're sitting on a chair, while you're driving, while you're soaking in the tub.

Most of all, I want you to not harm yourself. You may not like you, but Jesus loves you more than you could ever imagine. I want you to like the sex that God determined you to have and not do things your own selfish way.

Even if you're mad as all heck, yell at him! I did, and he didn't destroy me. Would you kill your child who was yelling at you? You would send him to his room to cool off and later clarify his anger. I was so angry at God for inventing marriage! It was the most stupid, senseless thing I had ever done. And guess what? It was his idea and his fault, or so I thought. I would never get married again! Later, within several years, I was remarried to a wonderful woman who I just celebrated eighteen years of happiness. How did I achieve that? By following his words and his will and not trying to have my own selfish way. What do I drive now? A black, full-size Chevy truck. My house is much larger than the one I was kicked out of, and God even let me have a swimming pool in the backyard!

CHAPTER 22

---◇◈◇---

The Amazing Lieutenant Sedan

He was a reserve in the Marines. He was a reserve in the San Jose police department. It seemed that no one wanted poor Johnny. Why couldn't he do a career in the Marines? Maybe full-time military? Was he not tough enough? And now, why wouldn't the police hire him, full-time? I guess Johnny would have to remain Reserve Officer Sedan or Reserve Marine Sedan. Poor Johnny. After years of bootlicking, his moment had arrived. At thirty-one years of age, he was hired as a full-time, sworn officer. Better late than never, and now he was out to make people fear him. He would study hard in order to get promoted. Any accomplishment would be noticed and brought up to higher command. He would also take his Marine status with him.

General Patton and General Washington would have been proud of this individual. All others would soon learn to fear the Amazing Lieutenant Sedan.

Have you ever notice someone trying to stand out, either in dressing or maybe talking louder than others in order to be noticed? Maybe it's the neighborhood punk who has his pants pulled way down showing his underwear for the whole world to see. I once went to Hawaii for a vacation. Everyone was wearing shorts with sandals. Maybe swimming trunks or something casual; proper attire for a vacation in the sun.

COURAGE AND LIGHT BEHIND THE BADGE

There was one middle-aged man who was wearing a cowboy hat, long-sleeved shirt, and cowboy boots. It seemed *Howdy Doody* from *Toy Story* forgot his swim trunks. He would proudly walk to the swimming pool bar and sit and have a drink. You see, he wanted to stand out. Everyone would notice him, maybe think he was a wealthy oil tycoon from Texas. Wait, if he was, wouldn't he be staying at the Hyatt? Here, he was with the little people. He could draw attention, and people would ask about his life on the range and branding cattle. He would not be ignored.

I was going to tell him about my experience with Roy Rogers and how I had worked at the same location as Virgil Earp. He didn't come here to talk about the Wild West and its lawmen.

He came to act out what is known as "the Peacock Theory."

The Peacock Theory is based on the bird. The Peacock has beautiful feathers that he spreads out. Other birds are dazzled by its beauty. Females immediately love the bird and want to have its baby. The feathers are spread to make the bird look several times larger than it actually is. But everyone knows when the peacock is around.

The cowboy was all hat and no cattle, according to Donald Trump. But he didn't care. If someone would have told him that he looked ridiculous, it wouldn't have bothered the dude because of a high and overimagined ego.

Before I start with the character of Lt. Sedan, I hope you watched the movie *Police Academy*, and if you haven't, I encourage you to do so. If you can remember the character of the academy, Lieutenant Harris, then you've can have a good picture of Lt. Sedan. In the movie, Lt. Harris is trying to fire all the recruits and hopefully get himself promoted to a higher level. The characters of both men in real life and Hollywood are remarkable. At the end, the recruits show their high standards, and Lt. Harris is shown to be quite silly.

Johnny Sedan would need to stand out like a peacock, and the academy dress hat would be his prop. A cigar always sticking out of his mouth would add to the effect. With the hat always on top of thinning hair, he would then explain his short stunt with the Marines. "Boo ya," or I mean, whatever they yell when they're dismissing. The cigar probably came from watching too many war movies with generals sucking on cigars. Also, he could approach officers not wearing their hats on traffic control and quote "the book" and order them to place it on their heads. Officers could then say, "Wow, he was in the Marines and goes by the book!" "The Peacock" would then drive away, smoking his cigar until the book no longer allowed smoking in patrol cars. "Hoo Ya!" This great man was then forced to exit the vehicle and lean against the car, puffing away in order to keep with the book.

Our academy hat was great for the academy and also formal functions and funerals where highly dressed officers dressed in respect to the occasion. But it was of little use on patrol. At the sheriff's department, the hat was not required on duty. However, with San Jose police, one was supposed to wear the garment when working traffic control. One could wear a short- or long-sleeved shirt, but if you put on your jacket on, you would have to put the dreaded tie on! Makes perfect sense, doesn't it?

At one time, one had to put his hat on if he conducted a car stop. Imagine, you're on a suspicious car stop, and instead of focusing on officer safety and visual of the suspects, you're now looking for where your hat is so the Peacock won't drive up and embarrass you in front of suspects who just committed an armed bank robbery.

The reason for this lame rule is because someone back in the day had been pulled over and probably fled when police got out. Later, in court, the defendants probably said that they didn't realize that the approaching officers were actually police, because they weren't wearing their hats. Then the book said one had to wear hats.

Have you ever been pulled over and felt that the officer was not police because he didn't have a hat on? Usually the red and blue lights, not to mention the blinding searchlights, give the officers away, every time. Even if they have their hats on, one could drive away and later say that you thought they may have been armed greyhound bus drivers, because the only ones who would wear that hat was either North Korean army or a greyhound bus driver. Back in the 1970s, Texaco gas station attendants had to wear a similar hat.

Want to know who the biggest, most powerful being of all time is of the Peacock Theory?

I'll give you one hint. It got him kicked out of heaven. Satan! This proud angel thought he was the most beautiful of all. He thought he was above God. One third of the angels followed him, and they got booted out as well. There were now demons, and they are very active in this world. But good news! There are two angels for every demon. That, my friends, is "backup."

Can a person suffering from Peacock Theory attend church? Yes. But they let everyone know they're attending. It's usually the largest, grandest church available. Maybe cameras and the news is notified. Does God shine on this individual? No, he hates proud, haughty people and honors the meek, who honor God and not themselves, and the humble, who acknowledge a higher supreme being.

The first time I met the Amazing Lieutenant Sedan was on a beautiful spring day on the east hillside of San Jose, near the Evergreen area of the Paul district. Construction had been going on on the newly built housing community. I was directing traffic at one intersection. There were other officers, who were reserve officers, working other intersections and directing traffic for the large eighteen-wheeler dirt trucks. The great sergeant-soon-to-be-lieutenant was driving an unmarked city car to the police academy as he was the sergeant academy host. He saw numerous officers not wearing their hats. This inflamed the Peacock, because the book said to wear the garment. All officers appeared as recruits as far as the sergeant was concerned.

Little did the sergeant know that I was a lateral from another department with two more years' experience as a sworn officer. Plus, I, being hired at twenty-three years of age, did not have to wait for middle age to approach before finally being hired. I did not have to bootlick in order to be a desired candidate.

The Great Gunny approached and said, "I'm the sergeant of the police academy. You get your hat on and tell your professional buddies to put their hats on as well." Wow! Nice meeting you too! He then did the unthinkable. Instead of waiting for me to direct him across the intersection, he drove through, on a red light, with no lights or siren, with a city vehicle. So let's play by the book. He violated two vehicle codes and endangered any motorists driving through on a green light. If I had followed him to the academy, I could have made out a ticket which he would have told me what to do with it. So now we have a misdemeanor which is subject to arrest. I could then walk into internal affairs and advise of a sergeant who committed two vehicle code violations and one misdemeanor. Still want to play by the book, Johnny?

All because I wasn't wearing my hat! Ridiculous!

So why didn't I take this action? I didn't think the department would do anything about it.

I needed to continue with traffic control so the taxpayers were not endangered. I wasn't interested in being a peacock. I would need to look over my shoulder for a very long time.

Workplace bullying, creating a hostile work environment was not on the radar for me on the police department at that time.

My next adventure with the peacock was when I was back on patrol and made a mistake to work on the midnight shift. Here, the incredible sergeant had many friends. Most were just afraid because they feared he would make lieutenant and would make their lives miserable.

I had been with the department for nine years and had brought an additional eight years from San Bernardino sheriff. That was a grand total of seventeen years of police service. I wore three-service stripes on the long shirt sleeve of my arm. Each service stripe indicates five years of service. I wore this shirt many times on day shift with no one complaining. The book stated one could wear a service stripe for five years of service, but it had to be with San Jose police.

The peacock saw me and immediately planned his work environment attack. He first confirmed my work history time with the department, finding that I had nine years. Our police union was working on changing this as we were hiring a lot of laterals who wanted their prior experience shown. It was only a signature away, and the book would be changed.

The peacock waited for a night when my sergeant was not on, and he would have to watch two districts with me working on the district. He made his move. "This is Sam 10. Meet with me immediately!" The request came over my MDT I met with peacock, who did not appreciate me showing off my stripes of service. He wanted my experience from the sheriff's office erased! He told me I was lying to the community! The book stated that I could only wear one stripe. I tried to convince him that I was a former deputy in the Wild West. I tried to explain that we had two Marines in my academy who needed training in order to become certified military police. The Peacock seemed unimpressed and only wanted to take two of my beautiful feathers away. He ordered me to take two stripes away. I took all three stripes off, because I had more experience than nine years.

I later questioned an older reserve officer who had six stripes on his arm. This individual had ridden with the Amazing Lieutenant for many years. A reserve officer has to ride only one time a month. So he would have one time a month for over thirty years. This would total out to a year and a half of full-time experience. Wasn't this lying to the public?

The reserve explained that Peacock always went by the book and not to take it personally.

Great, so when the order changed, the Peacock would hunt me down and order me to replace the proper amount of service stripes.

The order changed and remains so to this day. For the rest of my career, I waited for the Amazing Lieutenant Sedan to advise of the update. It never happened, so "By the Book Johnny" isn't really by the book. Only when it suits the Great Lieutenant and when it makes the Peacock more beautiful.

As a Christian, we are not to boast or make ourselves look better than we are. We are to remain humble. If we find ourselves as a supervisor in any workplace, we are to lead with authority and leadership, with a friendly attitude toward people who are less rank to us. We are to avoid a hostile workplace by lying in order to punish a subordinate in order to have employees fear and respect you and in order to get even with the subordinate.

"Boo-ya, ex-Marine, Boo-ya," or was that "hoo-ya" or something similar?

This chapter is to familiarize ourselves with the "peacocking" that happens everywhere. From the swimming pool area of Hawaii to the workplace, to the street hoodlum wanting to expose his underwear to the shock of the taxpayer driving down the street, and also the bullying that happens at the workplace to employees, to the attractive young females who are groped by people of great power. Let's make it a habit to expose these individuals and notify attorneys who are standing by and waiting for your call. Don't wait like I did and take it, but take action. There are simply too many amazing people and supervisors who are dying to meet your attorney. Operators are standing by.

CHAPTER 23

---⟡---

Suicide

Caution: The following chapter contains honest material where the spiritually narrow-minded may find confusing and hard to understand. Reader discretion is advised. Being overly educated and self-sufficient may confuse the reader even more.

"King 6, San Jose." I answered, "King 6." "Possible suicidal male at 11023 4th Street threatening to jump off the rooftop of the home. Fire and AMR are staging and standing by." I answered, "King 6 en route."

I had been to many suicides and attempts prior to this call. This was a possible jumper with no weapon involved. Because of the suicide in the Victorville jail years before, I promised God that I would take these a lot more seriously.

I was now working downtown San Jose on a swing shift beat. Downtown is filled with halfway houses with mentally dependent people who needed room and board care. The house in question that I would arrive at was a large three-story Victorian home built at the turn of the century. Actually, it was a drug counseling center with a living area. Counselors with their first names being "Doctor" worked here and were presumed to be the experts in suicide prevention and emergencies. But this was a different situation, and they needed help—police help.

I arrived and was directed to an outside staircase that led me to the rear area of the house. I noticed a man standing on the peak of the rooftop. He was looking down at the cement, three-stories below. I was not actually the primary unit but had been assigned to assist for backup. No one was saying anything to the man, so I took over.

"Hey! Before you do that, I just want you to know that you've been lied to." The man hesitated and seemed quite curious as to what I had to say. The man appeared to be Hispanic, and there was a large possibility that he would be Catholic. "I bet you're Catholic." The man responded that he was. I said, "So that means you, at least, believe in God." The man responded that he did. Incidentally, I'm not telling another joke. This is real life. I went on, "If you believe in God, you have to believe in Satan the great liar. Right this moment, you're listening to the great liar."

Now I had his attention, and he was not about to miss a great story. He then sat down and actually lit up a cigarette. I went on, "It's good that you have that cigarette, because it calms you down. I know how you're feeling right now. You feel like quitting, and Satan is showing you a quick and easy way to get out. But as a Catholic, you know this is a sin, and you may not necessarily move to a better, more peaceful place. Whenever I'm working underneath a car and something is not going in place and my arms are tiring, I feel like pushing that car off a cliff. The fact that there is oil dripping in my eyes adds to the misery. But I take a break and come back later, maybe the next day, and everything slips into place. You're at that place right now, and the voice in your head is telling you to end it. I'm not your best friend, because I only met you five minutes ago. But right now, I'm your only friend and you're calling it wrong. You have a drug problem, but it's nothing that you can't beat. You just need to take a break."

The man spoke to me for the first time. "You don't think I have the balls to jump."

I responded, "That's not what I'm worried about. What I'm worried about is that you don't have the balls to come down here and handle your problem. But I do know that you're a man. As men, we handle our problems, right? You're not in trouble, and if you just come down, I have to handcuff you and take you to emergency psych services. But then you'll be released shortly and you can start over.

No big deal. None of the people standing behind me will touch you. This will be just me and you."

Officer DeeDee Garcia was standing directly behind me and had a talent for teasing officers. She was an excellent officer and handled situations like a professional. But I could hear her say "ohh, boy" when I had told the man about not having the b---- to come down.

I kept talking, and the man was ending his cigarette. I asked if he had kids and who would watch them.

The man spoke, "I have five, and they're old enough to get along without me. I explained that when parents kill themselves, the kids have a tendency to do the same later in life when things go wrong.

I explained that I would have to tell his kids about him killing himself and that would not be fair for me or his kids. I explained that he was tying up fire and paramedics who needed to leave and be available for calls. I explained that it was three weeks before Christmas, which is a busy time for us.

I again asked him to just come down so I could get him help. He began talking, but I could not hear him.

I asked him to come closer so I could hear him. I told him that my hearing was bad due to explosions and gunfire. Officer Garcia was mocking me, saying, "Yea, he has to wear hearing aids." I decided to make a joke out of that in order to lighten the situation. I spoke, "You see what I have to put up with? Now just come down so we can both get away from her."

A word of advice: Don't ever joke about someone about to kill themselves. The devil likes this and sees it as an opening to start talking to you about suicide. I'll talk about that later.

The man stood up as he was finishing his cigarette and approached the roof peak. He threw his cigarette to the pavement below. It sparked in a lively manner as it hit the ground. I could feel the crowd of police behind me tense as we were about to witness the man splatter his head on the cement below. I kept screaming, "You're calling it wrong. I'm telling you; you're calling it wrong!"

Where was my spiritual backup? Maybe caught in traffic! Where was the Holy Spirit? Suddenly, the man turned and walked down the rooftop to my location. He submitted to being handcuffed and was driven for the help he would need. I had a feeling that was higher than high.

The Holy Spirit had finally come down and told Satan to split. The man was now free to listen to me.

Later, back in my car, the primary officer typed over his MDT, "Thanks. I owe you big time."

Let's slip into the spiritual world to see what was going on there at the moment. Imagine a voice goes off in your head and imagine a conversation. You think it's your own imagination, but it could be the Holy Spirit talking with you. Please don't think that it isn't, because this man had been listening to the demonic voice when he got onto the roof. When we pray, we do not wait for an actual voice to be audible but more of a spiritual thought. It could give us an answer, but it's easy to think that it was our own thought. I didn't have time, but I'm sure someone was praying for the man at the time. I imagine the prayer going to voice mail with the angel in the call center going out to lunch. Finally, the angel returns and finally forwards the call to the proper authority. This is what it feels like sometimes when I pray. But actually, the prayer is heard and actions immediately start taking place.

In reality, Jesus was standing right behind me the whole time without me knowing. Right when the man was about to jump, Jesus said, "Leave," and Satan split. The man was then able to listen to reality and came down. You see, a miracle had just happened.

Now, through prayer, if I was to ask Jesus why he waited for the last second to take action, he would have said, "I was right behind you all the time. I didn't want to interrupt a good story. Plus, I was enjoying watching you put all that energy into the whole thing. Well done, my faithful servant!"

After reading my book, you know a lot about me without having to actually meet me. You know I take things seriously but know how to lighten things up by joking. This keeps me out of a psych ward.

By reading the Bible, you get to know Jesus and how he responds. So let's finish the conversation which Jesus. Jesus responds, "I especially like the part about you being under the car, but can you do me a big favor?" "Sure, Lord," I responded. He goes on, "The next time you're under the car and the part won't fit in and you scrape your knuckles, can you keep my name and my Father's name out of the situation? We had no part in the mishap." I say, "Lord, I'm working on it, but Satan was making me say those terrible things. Sorry."

Suicide is a horrible thing to witness. Don't even joke about it if you're a first responder. Satan is very powerful, and he'll have you believe the act itself is funny. The following day, I asked Officer Garcia if she thought the man was going to jump or was just bluffing because of the way she was joking at the scene. She stated, "I knew the guy was going to jump." My point is, don't joke about an act that is basically demonic. Satan will come calling again.

About two years later, Officer Garcia was having an argument with her husband while at home and off duty. Officer Garcia went out onto the front porch of their home. Officer Garcia placed a gun up to her head and pulled the trigger. Officer Garcia was one of the finest officers I have ever got to work with.

She defused many disturbances with a patient understanding and warmth to her citizens. She was a Catholic but failed to listen to the Holy Spirit. Let me say this again, Satan is out there, and he knows when you're at your lowest, and he will talk to you.

I came back to work after a three-day weekend. I'll never forget reading the briefing room chalkboard: "Funeral services to be held on Thursday for Officer DeeDee Garcia." What happened?! She had been on my team; now she was no more.

Suicide is caused by many factors. I say this not as a psychologist but just a trained observer who has cut down several bodies. It's, at first, a loss of hope, maybe by a chemical imbalance which can be corrected by taking medication. It's a feeling of hopelessness with no clear solution ever in the future.

The person has no one to talk to, and everyday keeps getting darker.

I once worked at an extra side job for Parents United. These are adult people who have been molested as children and are receiving counseling. There are others who are molesters getting treatment as part of a court order. And then there are people who are both victim and later decided to become a violator to someone younger, smaller, and more innocent. These were the ones that I found to be the hardest to understand. I was working as the security police officer for their well-being. The people were not related as far as the crime was concerned. I was able to talk with these individuals and try to get insight on their lives and predicaments.

One woman told me of being so depressed, that the dark cloud stayed over her for several weeks.

Only by taking her medication could she begin to feel somewhat happy again.

Another male subject screamed out loud as he was in counseling in the group, describing himself being molested. He screamed that he would kill the man if that man had still been alive. However, I noticed that he had, in return, sexually assaulted another human being. Should that victim be allowed to kill him?

To this day, I cannot understand why a person who was so mistreated in life can turnaround and do the same evil act on another human being. It's as if an evil being is talking to the individual and talking him into doing the same evil act.

Child molestation is so evil that if placed in a prison, the inmates will kill that individual once they know what their crime is. While working back in the jail, these individuals had to be housed in protective custody. They had to be marched into the jail cafeteria and away from the general population.

Pick up any newspaper, and from time to time, one will read about a teacher molesting a student, a priest molesting a child, or a police officer having an affair with a police explorer. How about the White House or people who are now running for office?

We are only now discovering all the victims of sexual abuse after many years of silence.

Who do you think these violators are listening to? Every man or woman worships something. It's because we were designed for worship. Some worship their fame and power. Others worship their favorite team or player and these people are paid millions of dollars to either run with a ball or run to a ball or to hit a ball or catch a ball. I'm surprised that these people don't go to Marineland!

They actually have mammals or fish that can swim backwards and balance a ball on their noses!

All at once, they flip into the air and place a ball through a basket! And all they require is a bucketful of sardines! Imagine, one could buy a T-shirt with *Flipper* written on the back. Then all of mankind can see that your team is *Flipper*. Then a fight can break out in the parking lot with another loudmouth who happens to be a *Bubbles* team supporter.

Ever notice that when a person picks up an automatic weapon and kills a crowd of people, he will usually then kill himself? The voice will say, "Well done, but I need you to destroy yourself now!"

Usually, the victims are in a church or a country western concert where the singers are singing about God and America. How can one learn to *hate* these people? Is it the lyrics that are so hated by the shooter? They don't believe in Satan yet they listen to him, believing that it was their own idea that they came up with.

*****

Suicide Is Selfish

I was working swing shift on patrol in the Almaden Valley area of San Jose. There was a call of a woman having a problem with an adult daughter who had returned to the mother's apartment to a disturbance with the mother.

Gus Pinto was the primary officer with me as the backup. I arrived to see Gus talking with fire personnel as well as the mother. One thing I can't stand are police who get out of their car and advise the party that there is nothing that police can do. I live in a small city where police are famous for this tactic. Also, my small city police dispatchers tell me that they have no police to send because they are so busy. I'm led to feel like I am guilty of something and should go right down to city hall to demand a raise in officers' paychecks and more officers.

Anyway, I arrived at an apartment complex and walked up and heard Gus advising the woman that there was nothing police could do. The woman had advised that her daughter was an adult who was living in Sonora. Her daughter had chosen a life of putting drugs into her body and had been staying with other people who chose this lifestyle as well.

The daughter had come to the mother's apartment in San Jose and had locked her mother out of the apartment. I think Gus liked telling people about getting a thirty-day notice and making everything a landlord-tenant issue.

I felt like I could help the taxpayer. I asked the mother for the key to the apartment and also for permission to enter. Officer Nutson assisted me, as Gus did not like me taking over his call. I unlocked the door and began to open it but felt some resistance. I then noticed a chair had been placed against the door to further frustrate my entrance.

I got the door open and saw that the adult daughter was standing by the staircase and looking at me. I explained that I was just there to check on her well-being. She would not speak to me, so I moved closer. I then noticed that there was a rope attached to her neck and tied to the stair rail. This explained why she was not talking.

I immediately cut the rope and had fire paramedics come inside to try to revive the woman. She was pronounced dead. I waited over two hours in the apartment with the deceased for the coroner to arrive.

In that time, I sat at the kitchen table to complete my report and try to comprehend why anyone would have to act in this manner. Officer Pinto left the scene, probably to go to Denny's to fume over the fact that I had jumped his call and to calm his anger with a hamburger with cheese and onions and a large coke.

During this time, I thought about how hard it is to be a parent. The mother apparently had no husband.

She had lived alone in this apartment. The deceased daughter had left to be in Sonora with fellow drug addicts. The daughter probably ran out of both money and drugs and seemed to want someone to pay for her stupidity. Life was not going well for the daughter. Her mother would have to pay.

Before I get into drug use, I have to say that in elementary school and in fifth-grade health, they told us the importance of not using drugs. They explained how they would be addictive and ruin one's life. The life would lead to stealing in order to support the habit. This did not appeal to me at ten years of age, and I was convinced I would not use drugs. Then at twelve years of age, in junior high school, I noted students smoking marijuana in the handball courts. A few years later, kids in my neighborhood were using drugs. A known person to me began using the ever popular barbiturates and selling the product. A truck driver showed how he could take "whites" and drive his truck for days without sleep.

At twelve to sixteen years of age, I couldn't believe the stupidity of these people. As I awaited the coroner, I couldn't believe the stupidity of the deceased. Here I was again questioning the intelligence of mankind.

But the remarkability of selfishness in the final act of taking her life in her mother's house. The mother probably drove to a relative's home. The mother could never go back or live in her house. The mother had no husband, no daughter, no home, and would now be haunted by this memory for life! The demons in this world were high fiving each other because today had been a victorious day.

The hardest thing one can do in life is not being a police officer, soldier, or doctor. The hardest thing in life is being a parent. No question about it!

*****

Suicide Can Become a Popular Fad

When I wrote about Officer DeeDee Garcia taking her life over a domestic dispute, guess what? One of our motorcycle officers then went on to take his life as well. He also had domestic problem issues.

I believe he also had children.

A psychologist was assigned to attend our briefing to give support and recommendation. Her bottom line was this: "Suicide can become a popular fad. It happened with the CHP, and it can happen with the San Jose police. It stops here, and it stops now. Man up or woman up and get through life."

After that, our suicide problem stopped, at least for that time period. Most of you know of Whitney Houston's demise and how her daughter followed in her mother's actions. It also can become a generational curse or habit.

My final thought on suicide: "It stops here, and it stops now!"

CHAPTER 24

———◇◈◇———

More Exciting Adventures

When a bank robbery goes down, a series of events happens. I'm sure the bank robbers already know this and plan accordingly. If not, they should find another occupation, maybe a job. There is usually a car nearby for a quick getaway, usually a stolen car. Sometimes, the stolen car is driven a few blocks to another car so it confuses the situation even more by making the job even more challenging for the officer.

Usually, the command "stick 'em up" or "reach for the sky" is given out by the suspects. This indicates a bank robbery is being committed. The teller will try to give some type of tracking device. This is already known by the suspect. If you're thinking of robbing a bank, you probably won't be reading this book. By the time the call is given out to patrol, the suspects are now several blocks away.

For some unknown reason, patrol units still like racing to the bank with lights and siren activated. The officers may feel they can beat the suspects out of the parking lot, but one would have to be inside the parking lot in order for this to occur. If it's a silent alarm, this is something different.

One male robbed a bank and got into the back and laid down on the back seat of the car. A middle class female drove out of the bank parking lot with no one realizing that the description would now be a female aiding the suspect.

However, I came in late and from another district. I had lost my ability of tracking but was now assisted by a tracking device. It was almost like cheating, but I would take the pinch anyway. My needle told me to go left and left I went. Right and right I went. It was nowhere near the bank. With all the units now in bank's parking lot, I had the room to do my tracking. I was lead to a residential home where I would later learn that Grandma lived. Suspects had gone to Grandma's house to hide the money in a filing cabinet in the garage. Suspects immediately left so if anything happened, Grandma would go to jail. Nothing like a grateful grandson. He would not be invited for Thanksgiving dinner this year.

I radioed the information to my dispatcher with my electronic toy screaming in the background. Soon, all the units were en route to meet with me before I made contact. I felt so special and appreciated for my talent. I'm still waiting for a commendation on this one. The units arrived, and we learned of the true identity of the robber so we did not have to take Granny into custody.

This would have alerted the NAACP of the brutal police taking a poor black woman into custody for merely providing the misguided grandson a place to store the winnings until things cooled down.

Upon learning the identity of the robber, the detectives in robbery would then be able to obtain a warrant for the suspect.

*****

Another time an Asian male committed robbery from Wells Fargo. I was once again late coming from another district. The units got a blip from a tower which I had known to give a false reading. I did not want to argue over the radio so I allowed the units to discover their error on their own. I came in wide from the east foothill area and allowed the electronic needle show me the way. When the unit began giving the loud warning noise, I began to follow the arrow and notified dispatch of my position and direction of travel. Units were now screaming over to my position. I was so enticed by today's electronics that I forgot to use good officer safety measures. I pulled up behind the suspect's vehicle not realizing that he could get out and shoot me. I saw two bodies flash by me with guns drawn and realized these were detectives who had followed me in. The suspect was dragged out of the car and placed in handcuffs. I provided him with a soft rear seat until another unit could transport him. I opened a rear window down a few inches to further aid in his comfort. I advised him to skip the wieners and beans while in custody in order for him avoid any heartburn problems while visiting the main jail.

Sergeant Tom Murphy arrived, and he was completely pumped over the apprehension of suspect and recovery of money. He likes football, and it was as if his team had just won the super bowl. If he had slapped me on the back one more time, I was certain I would lose consciousness. I never got a commendation, but he did finally buy me dinner during the week. He had heard of me tracking while in the San Bernardino desert and now I was proving I could track in a cement jungle setting as well with the aid of electronics.

*****

Have you ever heard the saying "the nut doesn't fall far the tree"? I was about to experience stupidity firsthand from this delightful and heartwarming tale.

I was working an extra pay job which had consisted of me directing traffic for a street paving contractor.

While standing in the lane, I noticed a male climb into a 1955 Ford truck which had been converted to a four-wheel drive. The truck was no show piece and needed a paint job and body work. A male climbed into the truck which had been parked across the street and would interfere with the crew.

Instead of driving around the block and parking the truck in his apartment complex, he chose to drive over the cement barrier with a uniformed officer standing there. As you know, it's a citable offense to drive over a cement barrier. One really doesn't want to do this with a police officer standing there. I was even wearing my North Korean army hat on. Maybe he thought I was an armed greyhound bus driver.

I approached him in order to at least advise him of his error. He immediately started swearing at me by saying that I could f--- myself. Angered, I radioed for a patrol unit in order to issue him a citation.

He locked himself in the truck. With backup units, we got the door open and arrested him for resisting officers and the traffic violation. I was relieved that he was white so I would not be on the five o'clock news.

Apparently, he had called his dad because he was feeling like he was being picked on. When his dad arrived, I informed him of son's indiscretion and name calling, using profanity. The dad looked at me and said, "Well, why don't you f--- yourself?" I asked to see his identification, and he stated, "Once again, go f--- yourself!" The dad was then taken into custody and handcuffed and placed next to his son! He told his son, "Don't worry, at least they didn't impound the truck." The father and son looked so cute together while being driven away in the backseat of the patrol car.

The construction crew was mad at me for failing to direct traffic, but I had not intended to arrest the entire family. I went back to directing traffic. One construction crew member mentioned that he had grown up with a man who had bipolar issues and any kind of authority would set them off. Anyway, I did not warn the family to avoid the wieners and beans at the jail. They would need to learn this the hard way.

*****

More Amazing Adventures of the Peacock

If you will focus on the movie *Police Academy* once again and view in your mind Lt. Harris of the academy, remember that he tormented the recruits who later had to save his life. I'll even borrow the name of the character from the movie. Lt. Harrises appear in every walk of life. Wherever you work, one of these critters is not far from the CEO or commander or whatever the boss or working head may be. Bootlicking has gone on as long as man has existed in the workplace.

In downtown San Jose, there existed the Mexican consulate. Mexican nationals were camped out and waiting through the night in hopes of an appointment with the consulate in order to gain citizenship in the United States. During this time, residents were complaining because the building was located in an affluent part of neighborhood. It was top news at City Hall, and the chief was trying to appease City Hall. The chief also liked wearing the North Korean Army–styled hat.

The Peacock or Lt. Harris was only a sergeant at the time but aspired to become a lieutenant. A request was made for patrol to conduct patrol checks throughout the night. I was on the graveyard shift, so I conducted these checks every hour. Lt. Harris never made any checks during this time.

The chief came to work very early each day. At five a.m., he was known to be in his car, driving to work with the police radio on. This was an excellent time for the Peacock to show his beautiful feathers and a sure time to get noticed by the boss.

At 5:10 a.m., the radio sounded, "Control, Sam 10?" Sam 10 was his call sign. "I'll be checking the Mexican consulate and conducting a patrol check." The Peacock failed to say that it was his only time during the night; thus, having the chief believe that he had conducted these all night.

Several minutes went by before I heard from the Peacock again. "Control, Sam 10, the consulate checks quiet with no problems or difficulties." The dispatcher announced, "Copy, Sam 10." I wanted to respond, "Chief, did you copy? The Peacock just conducted a check of the consulate, and he apparently should be promoted as the next lieutenant. What a good man!" But instead, I kept off the radio. Surely the chief would see through the acting ability of the ex-Marine reserve.

Rumors and gossiping hurts people in every sense. They occur in churches and at the workplace. Want to know who the biggest gossipers are? It's at the police departments. Members' reputations are destroyed, especially from people who have rank. One's chances of being promoted or shifted to a special unit are thus eliminated.

Usually, members of rank refuse to engage in this childish behavior because we hope and pray for great integrity. We hope that management can see through their desire for "greatness." We need people who can lead in a mature nature.

Do you think the Peacock was a great gossiper or liar? If you were to answer yes, then you would be a great detective. I won't bore you with anymore Peacock stories because there are too many other great stories out there.

A great friend of the Peacock's was also an ex-Marine and had a family from Vietnam. I'm glad to report that I was taller and out-weighed him by thirty pounds. Finally, I was bigger than someone else.

I don't know why they promoted this individual and I don't want discuss diversity so let's just say that they promoted him.

Worse, he became my supervisor. I had to drive sixty-five miles to work and I would sometimes stop at In-N-Out Burger for lunch. I would order a burger with onions. The problem is that onions cause bad breath. To remedy this, I had a bottle of Listerine in my locker. Before briefing, I would use the mouthwash full strength, because the briefing room seats were close together and I wanted to show courtesy to my neighbor in the next seat.

Apparently, and unknown to me at the time, two unknown officers smelled the Listerine and felt that maybe I was drinking alcohol before work. Instead of either contacting me and voicing their concerns, they went to Sgt. Danang to report that I was an alcoholic. When a supervisor gets a report like this, they are to immediately make contact with the officer to substantiate the complaint.

If the member has been drinking, he is immediately sent home as he is unfit for duty. If not, confirm the false accusation and let the reporting members know the truth so an ugly rumor is avoided.

Instead, the sergeant chose to follow me around the district for two weeks, shadowing all my calls. I didn't think much of it at the time because I thought he just wanted to be my friend. After work and in the locker room, he would ask to see my pistol that I carried after work. This allowed him to get quite close to be in order to smell my breath.

One officer, who was a police union representative, asked Danang why he had been following me. He replied that two officers smelled alcohol on my breath and he was keeping an eye on me. Rumor started to fly, and two different districts heard the accusations against me before I even knew what I was being accused of. These were senior officers who knew me well and knew that I have never needed alcohol to get through a shift. It actually became a joke. Officer DeeDee Garcia saw me in the elevator and began laughing. She stated, "I guess you're a drunk now." Garcia explained to a younger officer who was present about the lies and rumors that go on with any police department through rumors.

The supervisor who was supposed to clarify the allegation was fueling it by going undercover as James Bond.

I questioned Agent 007 months later, and he explained that the two officers had smelled the Listerine and reported me. I asked him about his technique, and he explained, "Don't worry, you're okay!"

I know I'm okay; I don't need alcohol to get me through a shift. I asked for the names of the two cowards who felt I was drinking. He refused to tell me.

I have worked with many fine Marines who are still active and great officers. These were just two of the bad apples who had no business in supervision. The good news is, I came into law enforcement two years before the Peacock and I stayed two years after he retired. My goal was to survive and make the community safer while I was on the beat. He wasn't tough enough nor were his professional buddies to have me quit. Both were liars and both failed.

Boo-yaaa, ex-reserve marine, boo-yaaa . . . or was that hoo-ya?

For present and future officers in law enforcement, when things like these happen to you, don't man up to the situation. Get an attorney and let your union know. This is a mistake I made that I will always regret. Supervisors like these have deep emotional problems where bullying feeds their ego.

*****

W. ALAN OROK

One Happy Cambodian Family

On the east side of San Jose, there are a lot of low rent apartments for Cambodian families who may be living on financial assistance. These people have had a hard life in Cambodia and are trying to live in the United States. They also know how to defend themselves because of a prior hostile government.

Defending themselves is just another day of existing.

An African American felt that he needed to climb in the kitchen window in order to take whatever he could to sell for drugs. Once he got into the kitchen area, he was harassed by the tenant and grandfather who wanted the intruder out. Leroy must have felt anger toward the grandfather so it was easy enough to beat the old man up in order to obtain what he deserved in the apartment.

He left, and it had been a successful day for the drug addict.

The family did not like the intrusion and bought a shotgun in case Leroy returned. The gun was then loaded with 12 gauge shotgun shells. A few weeks later, Leroy returned through the window, and there was grandpa again. He quickly smashed grandpa over the head in order to stop the older man from harassing him.

What Leroy didn't know was Aunt Thea was in the process of picking up the shotgun in order to solve Leroy's drug problem, not to mention bad manners. When Aunt Thea met Leroy in the kitchen area, she knew a dangerous threat existed. She leveled the shotgun at Leroy and pulled the trigger.

In an instant, Leroy entered into that spiritual existence that I have been talking about. He probably had not believed in this spiritual world, but he was certainly seeing it now. With his resume in hand, Leroy was now being interviewed by the King of Kings.

I was logging on for a day shift patrol on the Eastside. I was immediately assigned to the crime scene in order to transport numerous witnesses to the homicide detective bureau for questioning. These witnesses consisted mostly of several younger children and the aunt.

I walked up to the crowded apartment and noticed all the shoes on the front porch. I immediately recognized this as an Asian tradition. The kids seemed happy and alert and probably felt that it was

192

just another day of survival. I noticed that Leroy was resting peacefully on his back in the kitchen. I won't mention the blood that that was present due to his demise.

The kids walked by the kitchen without looking at the body and went outside to put their shoes on.

I then transported these happy, chattering children to the police headquarters. You see, these children were used to surviving the horrific conditions in Cambodia. This was just an annoyance that interrupted their already busy day.

If you have put drugs into your body and are now addicted and need fast money, do not, and I mean *do not* break into a Cambodian residence.

Grandpa may look like an easy target but remember Grandma may be packing heat!

CHAPTER 25

———◈◈◈———

More Miracles

Whenever I see something that I think is a miracle, I will try to substantiate with another observer, preferably another police officer. A doctor would be another good witness because they're scientists and generally want some kind of physical proof. That's why in the Bible, the book of Luke is so effective. Luke was a doctor who followed Jesus around and recorded the events as he saw them.

So if you don't believe in the Bible and the book of Luke, you're calling a doctor a liar.

I believe that there is a large amount of energy in just thinking. Have you ever thought of someone that you haven't heard from in a long time and was just thinking about them, then within a few days, you receive a phone call from them, and you said, "I was just thinking of you"? This happens more than you think. Imagine how powerful prayer is when you are praying to the King of Kings. It's immediately heard; only it may take a long time to get an answer. And it may not be answered in the way we wanted or even understand. Many people have felt the power of prayer while surrounded by other people praying for a sick or injured patient. Many doctors have witnessed this and can't explain it. Imagine if you have a doctor's degree and can't understand something.

I was working day shift on the west side of San Jose on patrol. I received a 911 call. "Sam 3" was assigned to fill me as the secondary unit. I arrived and notified dispatch of my location. The address turned out to be a very tidy apartment complex, and the room number of the 911 came from an upstairs unit. Wayne was the secondary officer with me.

I knocked on the door but got no reply. I made contact at the room next door. A lady advised that there was an older woman living in the apartment. I asked if the woman was living alone or with someone else.

I was told that the woman lived alone. The woman did not own a car so there would be no way to determine if she were home or not.

I told Wayne that I was going to enter even if I had to break a window or force a door open. He agreed.

We took the screen off and saw that the window was open about one inch. Wayne yelled through the window and heard a faint voice saying she was in the bathroom. We slid the window open, and Wayne went in and unlocked the door for me. We then found Mary on the floor in a rear bathroom. She said that she fell and needed assistance in getting up. We helped to her feet and walked Mary into the living room to sit on the sofa.

Fire paramedics were called to check Mary out. When Mary got up, I found no extra phone on the ground.

I figured that she may have a medical alert chip which she could push in order to activate her 911 home phone.

I told Mary that it was good that she had the alert button chip with her.

Mary said that she did not have an alert button or an extra phone which she would have carried.

The only phone in her entire apartment was on the living room table, well away from the bathroom.

I asked Mary how she was able to call 911 through her phone. She said that she never called 911.

I radioed dispatch, who clarified that the 911 came from the phone on the coffee table with the same home phone number.

So Mary either called 911 from the living room and went into the bathroom to stage the incident or angelic intervention had something to do with it. Mary did not want us to call anyone; she didn't seem to want family attention and pity. Because of her age and disability, it's highly unlikely she would stage such a dramatic act.

This leaves only one thing—an angelic intervention. An angel had dialed 911 to the San Jose police department. There is no other explanation. Upon leaving, I confirmed with Officer Wayne, "I don't think she staged that. Do you?" Wayne replied no. I said, "You know, we just witnessed a miracle. Don't you?" Wayne agreed that we had just seen a miracle. "Wayne, you're my witness if anyone calls me crazy." Wayne agreed that I was not crazy.

Angels have appeared and helped people throughout the history of mankind. Angels have given warnings, given directions, walked people out of infernos uninjured. They have stopped people from stepping out into the street and into an oncoming car. They have comforted people who were trapped inside a crushed car until paramedics could arrive. They are here at God's will to assist God in his needs.

In the Bible, the Old Testament lists angels 108 times, and in the New Testament, 165 times. So they are very active in this world. They outnumber demons two to one, so we are in good shape. Remember that the next time a demon is trying to talk you into something.

EPILOGUE

───────◇◇◇───────

We have journeyed throughout the state of California in the various law enforcement agencies. From the hot humidity of Fresno with its foggy, winter gloomy days. To the openness of the desert with its afternoon winds and its beautiful star-filled nights. Not to mention the stifling heat in an underpowered Ford with a bulletproof vest. And then to the mild Mediterranean climate of San Jose with its cool sea breezes.

I have met some of the best people in law enforcement as well as some of the worst. I met heroes who would give their life for me to cowards who only wanted to hurt me and better themselves. From crazy lunatics who did not care about taking a life to dishonest thieves and their attorneys. From idiots who placed illegal drugs into their bodies to people wanting to just end it all.

Civilization needs a law-based structure in order to live in an unchaotic community. We are guarded by rules, laws, and a belief system. A world without law enforcement is a dangerous world. The policeman is the warrior who is holding it all together. Without them, we will return to the jungle with the strongest ruling the weak.

Whenever one is wearing a badge and a gun, he or she is obligated to enforce the law in a fair, unbiased manner without regard for race or belief system. One has to show empathy to victim's and feel and hurt with them.

Their world may have just been shattered, and justice must follow.

We are entering a society where people are not submitting to proper authority. I recommend that these people visit countries where justice is lacking and see what their world would be like without police. Sacramento police have a policy where one is expected to "comply and later complain" if they were treated inappropriately. Tracy police actually played this game with me when I had mentioned something to the paper about their ineffectiveness.

The officer who I believe committed the act got away with it but got arrested a few years later on an FBI sting.

Since that time, Tracy finally made a duty manual and has had several knowledgeable chiefs lead the department into a fine organization. At the writing of this book, the present chief of Tracy is a former chief of San Jose police and an excellent leader.

Let's teach our community to respect and comply with law enforcement. Bringing them up with hate and disrespect should be stopped. Placing illegal drugs into our bodies will do exactly what our fifth grade teachers told us it would do. It turns us into stealing, lying, and killing. Young men should be using their youth into learning a trade or going to school. Not being lazy and getting high. Communities would then have to find a way to house and feed these men when they should be solving their own problems without a full closet of excuses.

I have included a lot of my belief system and a better way to face problems. People need a duty manual to life just as well as a police department needs a duty manual. At ten years of age, I asked my mother for a Bible.

It was a King James Version, so the wording was difficult to understand. You'll notice a lot of King James Bibles, but they're on the coffee table in the living room. You see, no one reads them. Purchase an NIV version or any newer translation version. Start a plan where you will finish in one year. Get to know the Creator of the universe and his love, anger, and plans for a better life for you. Learn to recognize the voice of the "Great Deceiver" who is a former angel who wants to destroy you.

At fifty-five years of age, I retired from the San Jose police department. I stepped out of my occupation with no special awards or numerous medals to adore my uniform. My award awaits me in heaven, and it will be presented by my Lord and King. To end this book, I dedicate Psalm 104: 24–35. You'll have to look it up.

You are the investigator now. Stay safe!

This photo was taken in 1996 during San Jose Police community outreach/service- fishing in the park with the kids.

This Photo was taken in 1997 (while I was in San Jose's patrol car).

This is a photo of all of my badges.

ABOUT THE AUTHOR

Alan and his wife live in Central California, where he enjoys his retirement after thirty-two years of police work. He has two sons who live in the Los Angeles area, where one is enrolled at UCLA and the other from Riverside University. Both were not called to a career in law enforcement. Alan enjoys California where he can visit the desert, the beach, and the mountains all in the same day. He enjoys camping, fishing, and traveling to Bali and Hawaii, as well as his High Sierras. Alan enjoys the adventure of reading, as this allows him to battle the boredom of civilian life.

CPSIA information can be obtained
at www.ICGtesting.com
Printed in the USA
FSHW011945070420
68933FS